EXPLORING THE ANCIENT AND MEDIEVAL WORLDS

# Feudalism in Medieval Europe

Pliny O'Brian

Cavendish Square
New York

Published in 2016 by Cavendish Square Publishing, LLC
243 5th Avenue, Suite 136, New York, NY 10016



First Edition



Cataloging-in-Publication Data

O'Brian, Pliny.
Feudalism in medieval Europe / by Pliny O'Brian.
p. cm. — (Exploring the ancient and medieval worlds)
Includes index.
ISBN 978-1-50260-681-5 (hardcover) ISBN 978-1-50260-682-2 (ebook)
1. Civilization, Medieval — Juvenile literature. 2. Feudalism — Europe — History — Juvenile literature.
3. City and town life — Europe — History — To 1500 — Juvenile literature. I. O'Brian, Pliny. II. Title.
CB353.O25 2016
940'.09734—d23

Editorial Director: David McNamara
Editor: Amy Hayes
Copy Editor: Regina Murrell
Art Director: Jeff Talbot
Designers: Amy Greenan and Joseph Macri
Senior Production Manager: Jennifer Ryder-Talbot
Production Editor: Renni Johnson
Photo Research: J8 Media

The photographs in this book are used by permission and through the courtesy of: Walters Art Museum, Baltimore, USA/ Bridgeman Images, cover; Preto Perola/Shutterstock.com, cover and throughout; Jean de Courcy/Gety Images, 4; Public domain/File:Fernando I, rey de Castilla y León (Museo del Prado).jpg/Wikimedia Commons, 7; MPI/Getty Images, 8; Universal Images Group/Getty Images, 12; Leemage/Universal Images Group/Getty Images, 13; Look and Learn/Bridgeman Images, 16; Hulton Archive/Getty Images, 18; Universal History Archive/UIG/Getty Images, 21; Fine Art Images/Heritage Images/Getty Images, 23; Centre Historique des Archives Nationales, Paris, France/Bridgeman Images, 29; The Stapleton Collection/Bridgeman Images, 31; North Wind Picture Archives, 32; Rischgitz/Hulton Archive/Getty Images, 35; Hulton Archive/Getty Images, 36; Richard Philp, London/Bridgeman Images, 39; Universal History Archive/UIG/Getty Images, 42; Culture Club/Getty Images, 45; Public domain/File:A Chronicle of England - Page 204 - Richard Pardons His Brother John.jpg/Wikimedia Commons, 48; Leemage/Universal Images Group/Getty Images, 49; Bridgeman Images, 52; Musee Conde, Chantilly, France/Bridgeman Images, 55; Leemage/Universal Images Group/Getty Images, 60; Public domain/ File:PriseDeConstantinople1204PalmaLeJeune.jpg/Wikimedia Commons, 63; Public domain/File:Magna Carta (British Library Cotton MS Augustus II.106).jpg/Wikimedia Commons, 64; Dea/A. Dagli Orti/Getty Images, 66; Dea Picture Library/Getty Images, 69; De Agostini Picture Library/A. Dagli Orti/Bridgeman Images, 71; Pantheon/SuperStock, 72; Tangopaso/File:Head of statue of the king Saint-Louis (Louis IX) (exhibition Saint-Louis 2014-2015).jpg/Wikimedia Commons, 74; Archives Charmet/Bridgeman Images, 77; Antb/Shutterstock.com, 80; Walters Art Museum, Baltimore, USA/Bridgeman Images, 83; Livre des merveilles/File:Hayton et Clément V.jpeg/Wikimedia Commons, 86; Look and Learn/Bridgeman Images, 88; Mary Evans/Interfoto/Sammlung Rauch, 91; Fine Art Images/Heritage Images/Getty Images, 94; The Art Archive/SuperStock, 98; Universal History Archive/Getty Images, 99; Public domain/File:Władysław II Jagiełło King of Poland.jpg/Wikimedia Commons, 100; Museo de Firenze Com'era, Florence, Italy/Bridgeman Images, 101; Public domain/File:Defense of Baumburg in 1231 by Teutonic Knights.png/Wikimedia Commons, 102; Photo12/UIG/ Getty Images, 104; Prisma/UIG/Getty Images113; Universal History Archive/UIG/Getty Images, 115; Duncan Walker/ Getty Images, 117; DeAgostini/Getty Images, 120; Public domain/File:A Chronicle of England - Page 417 - The Earl of Warwick Submits to Queen Margaret.jpg/Wikimedia Commons, 124; Public domain/File:Edward IV Plantagenet.jpg/ Wikimedia Commons, 126; Apic/Hulton Fine Art Collection/Getty Images, 129; Public domain/File:Princes.jpg/Wikimedia Commons, 131; Photograph by Rama/File:Philippe le Hardi mg 1694.jpg/Wikimedia Commons, 134; Public domain/ Web Gallery of Art/File:Philip the good.jpg/Wikimedia Commons, 137; Mansell/Time Life Pictures/Getty Images, 139; Public domain/Web Gallery of Art/File:Mary of burgundy pocher.jpg/Wikimedia Commons, 141; Public domain/Google Cultural Institute/File:Barend van Orley - Portrait of Charles V - Google Art Project.jpg/Wikimedia Commons, 142.

Printed in the United States of America

# Contents

This illuminated miniature shows the looting of Jerusalem by Christian crusaders in 1099.

CHAPTER ONE

# Christian Expansion in Western Europe

By the eleventh century, the Christian church focused the armies of Europe under the banner of "just wars" for Christian expansion. With this holy calling, Christian forces began to reconquer the Iberian Peninsula, and Muslims were forced out of Europe. The Catholic Church also spread out into new territories in southern Italy and along the coast of the Baltic Sea.

A major feature of the ninth and tenth centuries CE had been the vulnerability of Western Europe to attack from all sides—from the north by Vikings, from the south by Islamic raiders, and from the east by Magyar horsemen. In the eleventh, twelfth, and thirteenth centuries CE, however, European armies took the offensive. They seldom presented a united front, but they had the same general purpose and several common characteristics. Their social basis was the feudal system, and their military success depended to a large extent on armored cavalrymen who enjoyed great status within feudalism. Another major unifying factor was religion. The Western Europeans were fervently Christian and Christian in a way that distinguished them from the Christianity of the Byzantine Empire of the eastern Mediterranean. In 1054 CE, the church based in Rome and the church based in **Constantinople** finally broke with each other. From then on, the Latin Christians of Western Europe were fighting for their own civilization.

The clearest example of the religious influence on politics and warfare lay in the **crusades**—wars fought with the blessing of the pope on behalf of Christianity. The original stated purpose of the crusades was to recover Jerusalem from Muslim control; the **First Crusade** was proclaimed in 1095 CE, and over the next three hundred years, successive kings and emperors launched invasions of various countries along the coast of the eastern Mediterranean. The intermingling of religion with warfare was perhaps best shown in the formation of orders of warrior monks, such as the **Knights Templar** and the **Knights Hospitaller**, who fought against the Islamic armies. Ultimately, however, the strength of the crusading ideal was not enough to make the enterprise succeed. By the fifteenth century CE, Islamic armies had destroyed all Christian enclaves in the Holy Land, ruined the Byzantine Empire, and begun advancing into southeastern Europe.

Although the Christians failed to secure Jerusalem, their campaigns elsewhere extended the borders of Christian Europe permanently in all directions. From Spain to the eastern Baltic and from southern Italy to Ireland, armored knights fought with the aim of defeating the enemies of the church and creating personal wealth and power for themselves. Even within European society, the church encouraged its warriors to attack those whose beliefs were different from the beliefs of the church.

## Christians Attack Spain

The most important Christian offensive against Islamic armies was in Spain, where the Muslim conquests of the eighth century CE had left only five small Christian kingdoms in the north of the Iberian Peninsula. From west to east, these were **León**, **Castile**, **Navarre**, **Aragon**, and Barcelona.

When the Muslim states started to disintegrate into civil war, the Christians seized their opportunity. The count of Barcelona sacked Córdoba in 1010 CE, while Sancho III, king of Navarre, seized a large part of Aragon from the Muslims. Sancho then conquered León and Castile, thereby creating a large, unified Christian kingdom in northern Spain. However, on Sancho's death in 1033 CE, his kingdom was divided up among his sons; Ferdinand I became king of Castile and, four years later, of León.

Ferdinand I is generally credited with starting the **Reconquista** (the reclamation of the Iberian Peninsula from the Muslims), a process

Ferdinand I was one of the first Christian kings of Spain.

that took four hundred years to complete. Crowned emperor of Spain in 1039 CE, Ferdinand extended his territory, first by adding Navarre (after defeating his brother in battle) and then by conquering Coimbra (part of modern **Portugal**). He also forced the Muslim rulers of Seville, Saragossa, and Toledo to pay him tribute.

When Ferdinand died in 1065 CE, one of his sons, Sancho II, became king of Castile, and another, Alfonso VI, became king of León. When Sancho was killed in 1072 CE, Alfonso VI became king of both Castile and León. He continued the offensive against the Muslim states and, in 1085 CE, captured Toledo.

However, the Reconquista was not a smooth process. Early Christian successes were greatly assisted by the civil war that divided the Muslim states after the eleventh-century-CE collapse of the **caliphate** in Córdoba. Many of the Christian gains were later reversed by Berber forces—the **Almoravids** and the **Almohads**—from northern Africa. Although the **Berbers** saved Islamic Spain for the time being, they were not welcomed by Spanish Muslims and were ultimately unable to stem the Christian tide.

In 1212, the kings of Castile and Aragon joined forces and defeated the Almohads at the Battle of Las Navas de Tolosa. The Almohads were soon driven out of Spain by a united Christian front. Córdoba, the Andalusian capital, fell to Castile in 1236, and Seville was taken in 1248. By the end of the thirteenth century, only a few Muslim enclaves around Cadiz and in Granada remained.

The Reconquista was no longer a matter solely for the Christian states of Iberia. The Catholic Church supported the campaign, and the pope gave it his blessing. The influential Cluny order established several important monasteries in Spain. Fortune hunters from all over Christendom were invited to defend the faith in Spain, and they went there in great numbers, eager to win (in God's name) large estates in former Muslim territory. One order of Christian warrior monks, the Templars, made an outstanding contribution. In 1143 CE, the king of Aragon granted the Templars "one-fifth of all conquered Saracen land."

## The Beginning of Christian Spain

After Ferdinand I united Castile and León in 1037 CE, the two kingdoms remained (for the most part) undivided until 1157 CE, when León once again became independent. Eventually, in 1230, the kingdoms were united once more when Ferdinand III of Castile (who had inherited his realm from his mother) also inherited León on the death of his father. For the next two centuries, Castile-León was one of the two great kingdoms of Spain. The realm included Asturias, Córdoba, Estremadura, Galicia, Jaén, and Seville.

To the east of the Iberian Peninsula, the kingdom of Aragon was inhabited by Catalans, who spoke a language closely related to the Provençal tongue of southern France. The Catalans first took control of Barcelona, Valencia, and the Balearic Islands. Later, with the help of mercenaries, they extended their sphere of influence across the Mediterranean as far as the Aegean Sea. The king of Aragon, while vying with Castile and León for all of Spain, ruled Sicily, Naples, and Sardinia.

King Ferdinand and Queen Isabella

Political unity in Spain increased steadily throughout the Middle Ages. Finally, in 1469, Ferdinand of Aragon married Isabella of Castile, a union that marked the emergence

## "Just" Wars

As the church became involved in warfare, it became prescriptive about how that warfare should be carried out. It developed a code of chivalry under which, for example, an aspirant knight had to spend the night before he received his title in religious meditation. There were also profound philosophical implications. The idea of a "just war" was modified to embrace the notion that war could be justified only if carried out in defense of Christendom. This idea—which won popular support very quickly—was open to interpretation; it could validate wars of conquest carried on outside a kingdom's borders, either to recapture territory or to attack as the best form of defense.

One particular initiative that the church sponsored was the "peace of God." Aimed at the warring feudal nobility, it required warriors to spare and protect the weaker members of society in general and widows, orphans, and priests in particular. The peace of God even laid down the times when battle could be waged, forbidding any fighting between Wednesday and Sunday evening. Anyone not adhering to this code of honor was deemed to be committing a mortal sin, and any violations were dealt with in special ecclesiastical courts. Although largely ignored, the peace of God was an example of the church trying to impose order on a warlike society.

of Spain as a great power. Isabella became queen of Castile in 1474, and Ferdinand became king of Aragon in 1479. Although Aragon and Castile did not formally unite—the monarchs exercised sovereign power in their own realms—the combined kingdoms were a formidable force in fifteenth-century Europe.

It was during the reigns of Ferdinand and Isabella that the Inquisition was established in Spain in 1478. The stated purpose of the Inquisition was to root out heresy, but it also served to reinforce the power of the "Catholic kings," as they were now called. Royal investigators, called Inquisitors, could inquire into the acts and beliefs of anyone they chose and, acting in the interests of both church and state, condemn the accused in secret hearings. They were usually assisted by informers, and all parties—royalty, inquisitors, and accusers—profited from the proceedings, sharing the confiscated property of the victims.

## Portugal Becomes Independent

Only Portugal escaped the drive toward unification. The region was conquered by Muslims in the eighth century CE but was retaken in 1064 CE by Ferdinand I, who made fiefs of the reconquered districts. In 1143 CE, Alfonso Henriques (son of Henry of **Burgundy**, count of Portugal) was accepted by the nobility as **Alfonso I**, king of Portugal. In 1179 CE, the pope recognized the independence of Portugal and granted Alfonso permission to extend his kingdom into Muslim regions. **Alfonso III** (ruled 1248–1279) expelled the last Muslims from Portugal and moved the capital from Coimbra to Lisbon.

## Italy

As the Reconquista proceeded, Christian armies were also making territorial gains in the Italian Peninsula. In the seventh century CE, the **Lombards**, a Germanic people, had become dominant in the north of the peninsula, while **Byzantium** controlled large areas of the south. This situation continued until 754 CE, when, at the invitation of the pope, the Franks under Pépin the Short and his son, **Charlemagne**, intervened and deposed the last Lombard king in 774 CE. They then established the Carolingian kingdom of Italy in the northern and central parts of the peninsula. Southern Italy was left as a hodgepodge of small autonomous kingdoms and some Byzantine strongholds.

In the ninth century CE, the southern Italian Peninsula was invaded by Saracens, a name derived from that of a northern Arabian tribal people and used increasingly in the Middle Ages for all Arab and

Islamic peoples. In 827 CE, the Saracens drove the Byzantines out of Sicily and established several important bases on the southern coast of Italy, threatening Rome itself.

Pope Leo IV asked for help from Louis II, the great-grandson of Charlemagne. Louis succeeded in stemming the Saracen advance for a time, but after his death in 875 CE, the Muslims took over the whole of Sicily and parts of southern Italy, compelling the popes to pay them tribute. In the north, a period of anarchy ensued, as several minor kings competed for power. This period was ended in 962 CE, when Otto I of Germany gained control of northern Italy and was crowned Holy Roman emperor by Pope John XII.

In southern Italy, Lombard princes were dominant until the Byzantines returned in the tenth century CE. The Byzantines restored the rule of the *basileus* (emperor) in Apulia and Calabria and made Bari the center of their power. The rest of southern Italy remained under Lombard control.

Around 1000 CE, Muslims were driven out of southern Italy but remained in Sicily, which became a magnificent center of Islamic culture; the splendor of the capital, Palermo, rivaled that of Cairo and Córdoba.

## Normans and Christians Unite

The **Normans** came from an area of northern France that had been granted to the Viking leader Rollo in 911 CE. In the eleventh century CE, the Normans emerged as some of the most aggressive warriors in Europe, combining the ruthlessness of their Viking forebears with a fierce (and self-interested) Christianity. At the start of the century, Pope Benedict VIII granted an audience to several Norman noblemen who were searching for new opportunities, perhaps even a new homeland. Benedict VIII sent them to southern Italy, where they fought Muslims, Byzantines, and each other—hiring themselves out to local rulers or operating independently. The most effective Norman was **Robert Guiscard**, who arrived in Italy around 1047 CE. Guiscard began his career as a bandit and ended it as the ruler of southern Italy. He supported the pope's struggle against the Holy Roman emperor, and in return, his military actions were given the status of holy wars. The pope legitimized Guiscard's conquests of

## El Cid Campeador

The spirit of the Reconquista was to some extent personified in **El Cid**, also known as El Cid Campeador (The Lord Champion). Born Rodrigo Díaz de Vivar around 1043 CE, he was the son of a minor nobleman and was educated in the court of Ferdinand I of Castile together with the king's eldest son, Sancho. When Sancho inherited the throne of Castile in 1065 CE, El Cid became the king's principal commander and played an important part in the campaign against the Muslim kingdom of Saragossa, which ended in Saragossa paying tribute to Castile.

A portrait of El Cid

When Sancho died on campaign in 1072 CE, his brother Alfonso VI, king of León, inherited the throne of Castile. El Cid transferred his allegiance to the new monarch and two years later married Alfonso's niece, Jimena. However, El Cid's tendency to act on his own initiative, even against the interests of the king, led to him being exiled by Alfonso in 1081 CE.

Essentially a soldier of fortune, El Cid had no scruples about enlisting in the army of the Muslim ruler of Saragossa. El Cid won several victories for Muslims, including one in 1084 CE against the Christian king of Aragon. He was eventually reconciled with Alfonso VI of Castile, who recalled him to help in the campaign against the Almoravids, Muslim Berbers from northern Africa who were beginning to enter the peninsula. In 1094 CE, El Cid conquered the great Muslim kingdom of Valencia and ruled it (nominally in Alfonso's name) until his death in 1099 CE.

Robert Guiscard

Apulia and Calabria and granted him Sicily—provided he could take it from the Muslims.

Guiscard invaded Sicily around 1060 CE but soon realized he could not take the island on his own. He sent for his brother, Roger, to take over the campaign, but it was more than thirty years before the Normans succeeded in driving out the Muslims. While Roger fought in Sicily, Robert consolidated his power in southern Italy, taking the Byzantine administrative center of Bari.

After the death of Robert Guiscard in 1085 CE, Roger united southern Italy and Sicily. The Norman rulers who succeeded Roger maintained the preexisting laws and administrative systems of the Roman Catholics, Muslims, and Byzantine Greeks on condition that each group recognized the authority of the ruler of Palermo.

The Normans achieved a synthesis of Christian and Islamic cultures and created a state with a level of sophistication and prosperity unmatched in the Christian world. When Roger II became king of Sicily in 1130 CE, he ruled the wealthiest realm in Western Europe. This great empire flourished until the thirteenth century.

Muslims then came under attack from the city-states of Genoa and Pisa, which built large fleets that challenged Islamic supremacy and brought the Balearic Islands, Corsica, and Sardinia back under Christian rule.

## Northern Europe

It was not just in southern Europe against Muslim states that Christian Europe expanded. Some of the Normans who had conquered England in 1066 CE took land in largely pagan Wales and Ireland. Also during the eleventh century CE, whole communities were set up along the

Baltic coast and between the Elbe and Oder rivers in a concerted drive by Germans to convert the pagan peoples of the region. A crusading order of monks, the Swordbrothers, was established in 1202. The warrior monks were to hold one-third of the territories of Livonia and Lettia for the bishop of Riga and defend Christians against pagan attack.

In 1230, the **Teutonic Knights** were established. This new order of warrior monks absorbed the Swordbrothers and went on to rule the entire Baltic coast, establishing their own state.

## The Crusades

The church used the idea of the crusades to protect its own beliefs. In parts of Europe, especially southern France around Toulouse, there was a common set of beliefs known as Catharism or Albigensianism. **Cathars** held that the world was evil and could be saved only by pure individuals. Their views were denounced as heretical by the church, and in 1209, Pope Innocent III preached a crusade against them. That crusade effectively became a war between Raymond, count of Toulouse, and church-backed forces under the leadership of **Simon de Montfort**, who was a French-born nobleman. The fighting was confused—the king of Aragon intervened, and Innocent III became worried by the ambitions of de Montfort. As a result, the Cathar heresy was not stamped out until 1229.

The importance of the crusading spirit in Europe is best illustrated by events that took place across the continent between 1210 and 1220. During that decade, crusaders fought heretics in France, Muslims in Spain, pagan Prussians and Livonians on the Baltic coast, and Byzantine and Bulgarian forces in Greece and in the Balkans.

## The Story of Robert Guiscard

Born in **Normandy** around 1015 CE, Robert Guiscard was a soldier of fortune. He acquired the name Guiscard in his early twenties at the start of his career in southern Italy. The name comes from the Old French *Viscart*, meaning "wily" or "fox." His flaxen hair and commanding height betrayed his Viking ancestry, while his bellicose voice and fiery eyes inspired terror in all his opponents. By the middle of the eleventh century CE, he was the undisputed leader of the Normans in southern Italy, and his position was further strengthened in 1058 CE when he married Sichelgaita, a Lombard princess. His new wife was a formidable woman; tall and strong, she was as power-hungry as her husband and just as willing to go into battle. In full armor, a contemporary historian recorded, she was "a fearsome sight."

In 1080 CE, on a campaign against the Byzantines, Robert and his Normans were all but vanquished at the Battle of Durazzo. However, just as defeat seemed inevitable and the Normans began to leave the field, Sichelgaita spurred on her horse to pursue the army, shouting at the top of her voice, "Stand and acquit yourselves like men!" Shamed by the example of a woman, the soldiers returned to the fight and were victorious.

Sichelgaita continued to accompany Robert on all his campaigns and was at his side when he died of fever in 1085 CE, during another sortie against the Byzantines. She survived her husband by only five years. Robert's career of ruthlessness and arrogance were fittingly commemorated in his epitaph: "Here lies Guiscard, the terror of the world."

Advances in farming such as the horse-drawn plow led to an increase in the production of food, which contributed to Europe's population growth.

CHAPTER TWO

# The Dawn of European Urbanization

Between around 800 and 1300 CE, the population of Europe more than doubled. The demography also changed; at the start of the period, most people lived in the countryside, but by the end, there had been significant migration to the cities.

Between the eleventh and the thirteenth centuries CE, Europe enjoyed a period of population growth and rising prosperity, accompanied by political expansion. The interplay among these three aspects of the period has been much debated by historians, but there can be little doubt that they were related.

Population figures for the Middle Ages are difficult to verify. In 800 CE, the empire of Charlemagne may have comprised fifteen million people, and there were probably another fifteen million in the rest of what is now known as Europe. By 1300, there had been a huge increase. Historians generally give a figure of between seventy million and one hundred million as Europe's population at that date. The population of England had risen from around one million in 1086 CE, the year of the Domesday survey, to around six million in 1300.

The most basic (and perhaps most important) reason for the increase was that the climate of Europe changed. Modern techniques enable historians to confirm that the climate warmed up during this period. Wine production took place in northern England (unthinkable today), while Scandinavian explorers were able to settle in Greenland—so named because crops could be cultivated there.

Climate change increased temperatures throughout Europe, which contributed to good harvests across the continent.

(The Scandinavian settlements in Greenland were later abandoned as the climate turned colder.) With warmer weather came larger crop yields and fewer bad harvests.

This climatic advantage was then boosted by improvements in the technology of farming. The agricultural techniques of the early Middle Ages were quite primitive, resulting in meager harvests. Peasants farming the land used crude wooden plowshares (cutting blades) that just ripped open the earth without turning it over. Sometimes, manure was thrown into the furrows before the seed was planted, but after that, farmers did no more than hope for favorable weather to encourage their crops to grow. The failure of a crop could result in famine. Most of the cattle were routinely slaughtered every fall because the land could not produce enough to feed them through the winter.

In the eleventh century CE, revolutionary new farming methods were introduced. The most important of these was the curved moldboard that was attached to the cutting blade of the plow; the device may have been adapted from a similar implement that had been used in the eastern provinces of the former Roman Empire. The improved plow not only cut into the earth but also turned it over, creating a much better environment for crop growth and resulting in much better yields. Another improvement was the horse collar (probably imported from Asia), which enabled horses instead of oxen to be used to pull plows. The collar, together with the introduction of iron horseshoes, resulted in a more efficient use of animal power.

There was a further range of technological advances that improved food production. Watermills and windmills made flour making more efficient than ever before (the first recorded windmill was in Yorkshire, England, in the late twelfth century).

Finally, a new system of crop rotation was adopted. The earlier practice had been to leave half of the fields fallow (unplanted) at any one time, to give the land time to recover. Under the new three-field system, one field was used for an early crop, another was used for a late crop, and the third was left fallow. This meant that more land was under cultivation, which, together with the other improvements, resulted in a marked increase in the food supply. The consequences of these developments were healthier nutrition in the populace at large, a greater life expectancy, and an increasing population.

Why these technological advances and better procedures should have come into being is again a matter of conjecture. It is almost certainly linked to the defeat of the raiders—Vikings, Magyars, and Saracens—who had previously hindered technological progress.

The church was also important in the development of farming. The **Cistercians**, a monastic order founded in 1098 CE, concentrated on manual labor. They depended on what they produced for their entire income and became great agriculturalists, leading the way in developing new techniques and (partly because they kept excellent records) refining the breeding of both horses and cattle.

The rising population needed new land, and there were great movements of people, both within their own localities and farther afield. Previously unused land was made productive; vacant swamplands were drained for cultivation and forests were cut down to make fields. Settlers also moved east to areas such as the Baltic region and set up new villages.

## Specialization and Textiles

In addition to producing better harvests, the agricultural innovations had another effect. The increased crop yields were achieved by fewer workers, so in the regions where the new techniques were most widely adopted, some people were released from basic agricultural production. Many of these people began to produce goods at home for sale.

Technical innovations improved the production of other goods, particularly textiles. Historically, most spinning and weaving had taken place in the large manor houses, and only enough cloth was produced to satisfy the needs of the residents. During the Middle Ages, a pedal loom (perhaps originally used in Asia) was introduced. Probably first employed extensively in **Flanders**, the pedal loom permitted much faster weaving and significantly increased output. Weavers using such looms produced more than enough cloth to satisfy their own needs and sold the rest. The increased production and availability of woven material stimulated demand for raw wool and spun thread; that demand, in turn, stimulated the wool trade.

The new breed of market-oriented weavers needed a ready outlet for their cloth and the finances to invest in new looms. As a result, the new textile industry became increasingly concentrated in cities. The new, urbanized industry became an important factor in the rise of commerce in a number of regions, particularly the Italian Peninsula and northwestern Europe, in the areas that are now Holland and Belgium.

## Fairs and Markets

A strong index of the increase in economic activity was the number of annual fairs that began to be held in Western Europe during the twelfth century to foster contact between merchants and facilitate business. Traders needed a central place to meet, and the most convenient location was on the plains of eastern France, in the region of Champagne. There, a cycle of large annual fairs was held, beginning in January at Lagny. Next, on the Tuesday before the middle of Lent, the city of Bar had its turn. That was followed by the market of Saint Quiriace, near Provins, while in June, the "hot market" (named for the weather at that time of year) took place at Troyes. In September, there was a second fair in Provins, and later in the fall, the season ended with a "cold market," which was convened in Troyes.

These annual fairs were attended by merchants from far and wide, and foreigners who came to trade were exempted from the provisions of local law. The count of Champagne guaranteed the free

Fourteenth-century fair at Westminster. Fairs were an essential part of the economy of Europe in the Middle Ages.

legal status of the merchants and sent soldiers to enforce his edict. This arrangement, the "market peace," was administered by market masters or bailiffs, of whom there were two, usually a nobleman and a merchant, both appointed by the count. The market masters issued permits to the notaries and moneychangers who served the public, and they appointed a small army of sergeants to maintain order.

These sergeants were often needed. Many competing merchants and buyers with different customs and languages met at the fairs, and arguments about prices, weights, and the quality of the merchandise were bound to erupt. Discipline was strict. Those who broke the rules were sure to fall into the hands of a sergeant and be dealt swift justice. The market tribunal had to pass judgment between sunrise and sunset, even in the most serious cases, and sentences were carried out immediately. The market masters sealed their sentences with personal seals similar to those used by cities and feudal lords; such seals were symbols of their autonomy.

The fairs were not merely trade fairs; they also had a festival atmosphere. They attracted magicians and other performers, troubadours (who sang the latest songs), and prostitutes (who did a thriving business). The wine flowed freely.

The fairs were such a success that they were eventually held throughout Europe, and some of them survive today as carnivals. In the thirteenth century, the commercial importance of the fairs declined, as merchants began to conduct their business from offices rather than travel long distances to trade fairs. It was no longer profitable to drag small quantities of merchandise around in wagons. If a merchant were rich enough, he might send representatives abroad to trade, carrying goods in ships that had become larger and more seaworthy. The new financial practices that had originated at the fairs now made extensive travel unnecessary.

## Banking and Moneychangers

A great deal of money changed hands at the fairs, and many different currencies circulated there, including Venetian coins, French livres from Tours, and British silver coins. Fairs were also flooded with the generally accepted coinage of the city of Provins, minted by the count of Champagne. It was difficult for the ordinary person to understand the value of the various currencies, particularly when a great deal of questionable money was circulated. Most merchants wanted to get their hands on a currency that would be accepted at home.

That is where the moneychangers came in. Sitting behind benches piled with a variety of currencies, they used scales to weigh the coins offered by merchants and exchanged the money for a more acceptable currency, keeping a small percentage of the amount as a fee. The value of a coin was determined by the weight of the precious metal used to make it. The system worked well, unless a moneychanger was dishonest and used false weights on his scales to increase his profits. The penalties for such practices were severe. Convicted cheats lost all their possessions, and their benches were broken up. Expressed in Italian, this was *banco* (bench) *rotto* (broken), giving rise to the English word bankrupt.

Merchants needed a great deal of money at the fairs, but it was dangerous to travel with bags of gold. A method of money exchange

Quentin Massys's *The Moneylender and His Wife*

developed, which avoided the need to carry large amounts of cash. This was the bill of exchange. It worked like this: if merchant A needed to pay merchant B a certain amount of money but did not have the cash with him, he would get a notary to draft a document (which was, in effect, an "I owe you," or IOU) in which merchant A promised to pay merchant B the amount in question on a certain date and at a certain location (for example, at Troyes during the cold market).

The process was taken a step further when merchant A no longer mentioned merchant B by name in his IOU. Instead, merchant A would simply promise to pay the amount at a certain date and location to the bearer of the bill of exchange. If merchant B wanted his money earlier than the date specified, he could sell the bill of exchange to another merchant for an amount slightly less than its face value (the amount stated in the bill). Moneychangers became eager to trade in these bills of exchange; because they were familiar with financial matters, they were able to make good profits on them. As a full-scale bill-of-exchange market developed, people were prepared to offer a price close to the face value of a bill as the day of payment drew near. Because anyone accepting a bill of exchange in return for goods could now cash it in almost immediately (if he was prepared to discount it), this greatly facilitated trade.

That was the beginning of the modern banking business. A number of moneychangers moved from the fairs (with their scales and piles of different coins on benches) to the cities, where they made profits from coin exchange and from trading in bills of exchange. They also began to lend money at interest, a practice called usury, which was condemned by the church because it entailed making a profit without work. As a result, the credit industry was conducted exclusively by Jews for a long time, until the church modified its view of moneylending and granted the inhabitants of Lombardy the right to lend money without it being a sin.

Some families in the northern Italian cities dominated in moneylending and soon became the most important financial dealers in Europe. They called themselves "bankers," and even kings borrowed money from them. In the 1330s, the English king **Edward III** borrowed large amounts of money from Florentine banks, putting up his crown as collateral for the loans.

## Trade and Growth

As trade and movement across Europe increased, luxury goods became important for the nobility. Many noblemen felt that it was essential for them to demonstrate their status, and there were soon many more goods available for them to purchase. Those lords who had been on the crusades to the Middle East wanted to bring some of the luxuries that they had seen in the Islamic world back home to their own castles.

So, there were many reasons why trade networks grew up—reasons concerning why goods were produced; reasons concerning why people wanted them; and reasons concerning the institutions and methods, such as fairs and banking, that made trade possible or easier. The result of the growth in trade was that towns became very important within the medieval economy. Towns grew all over Europe, but the most important areas were in northern Italy and parts of the **Holy Roman Empire**.

In northern Europe, a confederation of trading towns and cities, known as the **Hanseatic League**, formed by the late twelfth century. The Hanseatic League eventually spread its influence across the Baltic and North Seas.

## New Settlements and Communes

Many cities of medieval Europe had been founded in the Roman era, but with the population moving away from the land in the tenth century CE, new settlements sprang up. Traveling merchants established stopping places along their routes and built more or less permanent homes, and sometimes, small warehouses. Other people then flocked to the new settlements, which were often located at the mouth of a river, near a castle, or outside an old cathedral city, where the incomers might make a living providing services at church residences. Some of these new urbanites were former peasants, some were merchants, and others were artisans and masons.

The rise of the new settlements eliminated the need for the old relationship between landlord and tenant, and urban residents began agitating for changes in the law that reflected the new social realities. Ultimately, they achieved their aims.

By the twelfth century, the most influential townspeople, who were generally the merchants, banded together to oppose the taxes that were demanded by local landowners. The merchants also demanded the freedom to own property in the town without having to pay feudal dues and the right to self-government. Gradually, concessions were granted by the landowners, some of whom were pressured by rioting and others of whom realized that the prosperity of the town would be to their advantage. As a result, some towns were eventually granted charters by the landowners.

When a charter was granted, it often recognized a preexisting commune, the term given to the city's local government, which could collect taxes and administer its own justice.

A distinguishing feature of the commune was the oath taken by its members that bound them to assist and protect each other. Democracy was almost nonexistent in the commune movement. Almost everywhere, the rich immediately took exclusive control of the governing body and served only their own interests. The way the communes operated is exemplified in two very different cities of the Italian Peninsula—Pisa and Rome.

## Pisa

Pisa is situated on the Arno River, near the sea, and a road connects it to the coastal town of Porto Pisano (port of Pisa). In the early Middle

Ages, the population of Pisa was easily contained within the city's walls, which survived from the Roman era.

In the ninth century CE, a naval base had been established at Pisa to guard against the raids of Saracen pirates. As the Pisans gained control over the surrounding region and Christian culture flourished, Pisa's power grew rapidly. The fact that a Christian fleet was anchored at its port gave Pisa an advantage over other settlements in the area, while the presence of a bishop made Pisa an important religious center.

Throughout the eleventh century CE, the port and city continued to grow. By 1100 CE, Pisa had between twelve thousand and fifteen thousand inhabitants, an enormous number for those days. Its population was exceeded only by Venice and Rome in all of western Christendom. Pisa became such an important commercial center that the emperor gave it permission to mint its own coins.

However, by the twelfth century, Pisa was no longer the only urban center in the region; Genoa to the north and Florence to the east had become significant rivals. The Pisans were almost constantly at war with the Genoese, another maritime power, while inland, the Florentines were a perpetual threat. Eventually, Pisa was put on the defensive when its possessions of Corsica and Sardinia, once wrested from the Muslims, were conquered by the Genoese, and in the late thirteenth century, Pisa gradually diminished into a second-class power.

From the evidence of a contemporary document written by the bishop of Pisa, in which he mentions "consuls," it appears that communal government may have existed in Pisa from the end of the eleventh century CE. Under communal governments, consuls were magistrates with a duty to settle trade disputes. When the commune was officially granted a charter in 1142 CE, it already largely controlled the city government, and its powers continued to grow. In 1165 CE, a paid chancellor was appointed to serve the council, and in the same year, the consuls introduced the use of a town seal. Power, however, remained in the hands of a select group of families that controlled all the offices.

The position of consul was unpaid and demanding. The entire city government revolved around the council of consuls, which had the final word on everything. Although a forty-member senate was established to function as a kind of advisory board to the council, the actions of the consuls were seldom closely monitored because the council also

## Monastic Poverty

In feudal times, monasteries played an increasingly important role in Western European society. Because people donated so much to monastic communities, such foundations became very rich, and the lifestyle of the monks was transformed from its traditional simplicity into something resembling that of wealthy landowners.

Such materialism was at odds with the precepts of Saint Benedict, who had dictated that every monk should live a life of poverty. The eleventh century CE saw the start of a movement by monks and nuns who were dissatisfied with what they saw as a violation of spiritual purity and wanted to return to the conditions of the early church. They went out into the wilderness to found their own religious orders.

One of these monks was Bruno of Cologne, who founded the small order of the **Carthusians** in eastern France at the end of the eleventh century CE. This was a very austere order, in which the monks lived in groups of around twelve—worshipping together but otherwise living like hermits in their own huts. Abiding by strict rules of asceticism, the Carthusians lived in poverty, silence, and solitude. The order did not become popular until the late fourteenth century.

A more appealing order was that of the Cistercians, founded in 1098 CE by Robert, a Benedictine abbot. After an abbey dispute over the interpretation of the rule of Saint Benedict, Robert took some followers to Citeaux in Burgundy, where they set about reclaiming the wilderness for cultivation. They built a **monastery** with its own rules for an austere and simple life. The monks tilled the land, ate a frugal diet of black bread and stewed vegetables, and did not speak unless it was absolutely necessary. This type of monastic life attracted many people, and by 1250, there were some 750 Cistercian monasteries across Europe. To prevent the monasteries from becoming rich, it was decided that the only gift the communities could accept was uncultivated land. In devising ways to make these lands productive, the Cistercians contributed greatly to Europe's economic development.

appointed the senators. If there were any criticisms of the government, they were aired in the city parliament, which was open to all citizens.

This system did not last for long. Infighting tore the oligarchy (government by an elite) apart, while groups of citizens who had no power demanded reforms. In the thirteenth century, the Pisans brought in a **podesta** (hired strongman) to govern the city and assure peace. By that time, relationships within the urban oligarchies throughout Italy had degenerated to such an extent that city government suffered as a result. In Pisa, the various rulers did quite a good job, gradually reducing the influence of the council of consuls. Even so, the typical podesta concerned himself only with the interests of the old oligarchy and, consequently, did not enjoy the trust of the middle classes (the merchants and artisans of the **guilds**). In the second half of the thirteenth century, these guilds controlled Pisa. Ultimately, all parties lost out. In the fourteenth century, many Italian cities fell into the hands of unscrupulous men who either pushed aside the governing bodies or made them puppet administrations.

## The Commune of Rome

Another example of the troubled development of a commune is Rome. For centuries, Rome had been a bone of contention among local aristocratic families, kings, and clerics. Rome had the largest clerical organization in all Christendom, so it remained a large city even though its lay population had been drastically reduced in previous centuries. The city's main source of income was the countless pilgrims who visited the papal residence. However, although trade revived and the population increased substantially, Rome never became an important commercial center; it remained primarily a city of pilgrims and priests.

Nevertheless, there was widespread dissatisfaction with the rule of the pope and the prefect who served as the pope's top official. The dissatisfaction came to a head in 1143 CE, when there was a popular uprising and a communal government was established that the people proudly referred to as their senate, evoking the memory of the ancient senate of the Roman republic. A city parliament similar to the one in Pisa chose fifty senators—forty of whom monitored policy, while ten

Charter of the Peronne Commune

*ordinarii* (ordinary men), who held office for only six months, constituted the actual government. The senators acted with great self-confidence; they even minted coins bearing the initials SPQR, which had been used by the Roman Empire and stood for *senatus populusque Romanus* (the senate and the people of Rome).

The senate forced Pope Eugenius III (ruled 1145–1153 CE) to leave the city in 1146 CE. The pope continued to fight the new Roman republic from the country, but he was unable to return to the city until 1148 CE. Meanwhile, the situation in Rome became so critical that the senators appointed a *patricius* with almost dictatorial powers to maintain their freedom. However, it was a vain effort. The people eventually lost most of what they had gained; although the senate continued, the pope began to appoint all its members.

Tension mounted whenever **Arnold of Brescia** (see box, page 31) appeared on the streets of Rome. He was a fervent religious reformer and inflamed the feelings of the Roman populace by speaking out against the corruption in the church and the extent of the pope's temporal powers. His sermons advocating a church independent of worldly rule were received enthusiastically by supporters of the old senate.

During another uprising, Arnold promptly joined the rebels. A crowd of around two thousand people appointed one hundred senators and two consuls, and the new senate promptly elected an emperor. The people's emperor constituted a dangerous precedent for the pope and the Holy Roman emperor; not only did the appointment of a people's emperor flout the pope's right to crown and control the temporal ruler, it also threatened the established order. Consequently, the city lost the support of the antipapal nobles and stood alone.

When an Englishman named Nicholas Brakespear became Pope Hadrian IV (ruled 1154–1159 CE), he was not disposed to compromise with rebels. In 1155 CE, he made a pact with the German emperor, **Frederick I (Barbarossa)**, and put Rome under an **interdict** (in effect, a mass excommunication that prohibited carrying out any of the sacraments, including Christian burial). The interdict upset the population, and the closer Barbarossa's troops came to the city, the more support the senate lost. The faithful began to demand that Arnold be sacrificed. Deprived of senate protection, Arnold fell into the hands of Frederick. Arnold was tried and condemned for heresy and was executed by hanging.

The Roman commune ended in 1198 CE, when Pope Innocent III (ruled 1198–1216 CE) acknowledged the legality of the prefect and the senate, but with the provisos that the pope would have ultimate control and the prefect would rule according to his wishes. The Romans were apparently satisfied with this compromise, and the system functioned satisfactorily for many years.

## City-States Continue to Grow

Throughout most of Europe, the developing cities gradually won charters from their overlords. Under those charters, the cities were granted self-government in exchange for an annual tax or tribute paid to the landowners. However, the amount of "freedom" varied, and most cities still came under laws laid down by a king or an emperor. In the Holy Roman Empire, some fifty cities succeeded in achieving almost complete independence, but many others retained close ties with traditional rulers.

Italy was the foremost developer of city-states, many of which were formed in the region between the Alps and the Tiber River. Lombardy became a patchwork of small autonomous city-states that dominated the surrounding countryside. However, the main Italian cities were large, dwarfing in size other European cities. In the German Empire, for example, Frankfurt, with its nine thousand inhabitants, was considered an enormous city, but a population of that size in Italy was not unusual. Only capitals such as London and Paris,

## Arnold of Brescia

Arnold of Brescia (ca. 1100–1155 CE) was a monk who became abbot of the monastery in Brescia, where he became notorious for his outspoken condemnation of the corruption rife in the church and for his proposals for reform. He was sharply critical of the wealth of the church and demanded that the clergy give up its political role and apply itself to spiritual care. He earned the condemnation of Pope Innocent II, who exiled him from Italy in 1139 CE.

Arnold took refuge in France, where he became a student of the famous philosopher, Peter Abelard. Arnold continued to preach until he was exiled from France in 1141 CE, having been condemned as a heretic. Arnold escaped again, this time to Switzerland and then to Germany. In 1145 CE, he was reconciled with Pope Eugenius III and allowed to return to Rome.

From that time onward, Arnold was at the forefront of the radical movement in Rome, and when Pope Hadrian IV and Emperor Frederick I (Barbarossa) made a concerted effort to put down the rebels, Arnold became the scapegoat. Condemned for heresy by an ecclesiastical court, he was handed over to the emperor for execution in 1155 CE.

Arnold of Brescia preaches to a captivated crowd.

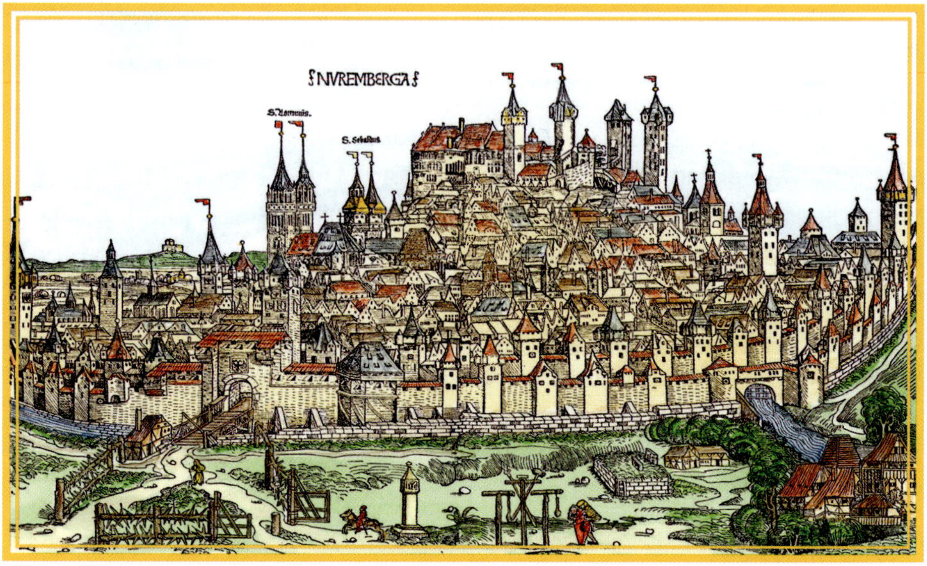


Nuremburg was surrounded by a wall that served as a form of defense.

and economic centers such as Ghent and Bruges, could compare in size with the Italian metropolises.

The large cities were fully able to defend themselves against aggressors, but for small cities, war meant withdrawing behind the ramparts and hoping for a quick end to the conflict. Most urban citizens were not interested in trying to extend their political power. They wanted merely to carry on their lives and work in peace and quiet. They also wanted the safe roads and economic stability that were essential for trade. Any territorial sovereign who could satisfy those requirements found natural allies in these small cities.

Most of the earliest cities had started as settlements and then gained city status through a series of concessions on the part of the landowner. Toward the end of the eleventh century CE, the rights and obligations defining that status were fairly consistent across northern Europe. First and foremost was the right to make laws within the city. Permission to build walls around the city was also important, as were the governmental regulations that determined the precise extent of a landowner's power. A package of privileges, such as exemption from tolls, was often added.

Citizenship was another big issue. The citizens were free of traditional feudal commitments, so in theory, everyone was equal.

## St. Francis and the Begging Friars

During the twelfth century in Europe, some individuals began to adopt what was called the *vita apostolica* (apostolic life) in reaction to the growing wealth they saw around them—particularly that of the church. Under this concept, individuals took up what they considered to be the life of the disciples of Christ—a life based on simplicity, lack of possessions, and begging for food and shelter while traveling and preaching. However, groups of beggars claiming to be divinely inspired did not correspond with the prevailing customs of the church, and the fact that the mendicant (begging) monks were preaching caused great indignation because only priests were traditionally allowed to preach. Many of the itinerant monks were persecuted as heretics.

Around 1200, Francis of Assisi developed a more formal order of mendicant friars. Francis was a rich merchant's son who, after recovering from a serious illness during which he had several visions, decided that he would dedicate his life to solitude, poverty, and service to the poor. He cast off his fine clothes, dressed himself in rags, and—to the consternation of his father—spent the next few years ministering to the poor and the lepers who lived around Assisi. He also began preaching, even though he was a layman.

In 1209, Francis, together with a group of his disciples, traveled to Rome to seek the blessing of the pope, Innocent III, himself a deeply pious man. The pope approved Francis's ideas, finding them unusual but not heretical. Soon, Francis had many followers, who traveled on foot throughout Italy, preaching and ministering to the poor.

Other mendicant orders, such as the Dominicans (founded by Saint Dominic), were established throughout Europe over the following decades.

Consequently, the city was usually an excellent refuge for runaway serfs. There was an almost universal rule that anyone who had lived for a year and a day in a city was considered free, and most city dwellers were supportive of runaways. Some lords actually founded cities with a charter that expressly incorporated the year-and-a-day rule, specifically to attract serfs from rural estates. However, the same lords ensured that their own serfs did not benefit from similar dispensations.

The rights of any particular city were rarely unique. In general, a landowner would grant privileges that were already in effect in other cities. The whole package of rights and regulations making up the urban laws was called the city charter. The details of the charter were inscribed on parchment, and its terms were recognized by the law of the realm. The charter document was kept in the municipal archives, and many European cities still have their original charters today.

## Medieval Guilds

Inside the city walls, there were many artisans practicing different crafts and trades, and by the eleventh century CE, most craftsmen were united in guilds. The very earliest guilds were formed by wealthy merchants who banded together to secure an urban charter from their landowner. These politically motivated guilds often survived as a necessary component of urban government. Other guilds were formed as clubs or societies whose members celebrated certain festivities together. These clubs and societies eventually evolved into associations for members of particular trades and became the medieval guilds.

The guild was an important instrument in regulating the practice of any particular craft. The guild, or more particularly the masters of the guild, laid down the conditions of trade (which only members of the guild were allowed to practice), established the prices of the goods, and set standards for the quality of the products, the techniques to be used, and the maximum size of the shops in which the goods were sold. The guild masters made sure that the members adhered to the rules.

The guilds also functioned as schools for their respective crafts. A boy wanting to learn a particular trade would apply to a master to be hired as an apprentice. Apprenticeships might last as long as seven years, but once the apprentice became proficient in his craft,

Glassblowers would learn their skills by apprenticing to masters through a guild.

he could be promoted to journeyman. A journeyman worked for a master for a daily wage, and with this additional experience, he might be made a master, which gave him the right to start his own business. In the fourteenth century, it was customary for the journeyman to take a kind of exam. He had to produce a "masterpiece," which was judged by the masters of the guild. If the work was considered of sufficient merit, the journeyman was promoted to master.

The guild masters could regulate the size of the trade group; they could keep the number of small businesses in check by promoting only a few journeymen to master. It was not uncommon for an excellent craftsman to rise no higher than journeyman because the masters thought there were already enough masters in the craft in the city. Although it was possible for a craftsman to join a guild in another city, he would not be allowed to start his own business there; outsiders were prevented by law from doing so. That situation prevailed until the late eighteenth century, when the French Revolution put an end to the guild system in most of Europe.

The guilds were important as social clubs, and the guild halls would hold wild parties for the guild members. Guilds also vied to stage the most impressive processions and competed with each other over the chapels they designed for the sidewalls of the churches. Guild chapels were used by members both for worship and for meetings.

William I, who invaded from Normandy to become king of England

# CHAPTER THREE

# The French and the English

The eleventh and twelfth centuries CE saw the transformation of France from a geographical area into a cohesive and powerful state. During the same period, England moved out of the Scandinavian sphere of influence and became a European power.

During the eleventh and twelfth centuries CE, there were major structural changes in the governmental systems of France and England. In France, the feudal system was breaking down, giving way to a strong monarch at the head of an effective bureaucracy. In England, a centralized state emerged, with a well-organized administrative system.

## France Transforms

After the death of Charles the Bald in 877 CE, the three kingdoms of Francia, set up under the Treaty of Verdun in 843 CE, became increasingly weaker. Throughout the succeeding century, the kings did little more than play off their troublesome vassals against each other, a practice that often backfired on them. Whenever a competing royal family appeared on the scene, it could always find partisans to support it, and divisiveness became entrenched. The empire turned into a chaos of bickering baronies.

The barons had no interest in electing a powerful king, so they had no trouble, in 987 CE, in accepting **Hugh Capet**, a scion of the royal family of Robertines. His father was Hugh the Great, lord of most of northern France and count of Paris, and his mother was Hadewig, a sister of Holy Roman Emperor Otto I. Hugh Capet's sphere of influence in France extended only from Paris to **Orléans**, and even in this narrow corridor, his power was challenged by rebellious members of the western Frankish nobility. For Capet, kingship was little more than the crown on his head, and he did not attempt to extend his sway beyond his own territory.

Hugh Capet's successors followed his example, inconspicuously strengthening their position in the domain. It took two centuries for this patience and realism to produce tangible results, but it finally did so under **Philip II Augustus** (ruled 1180–1223 CE). Philip expanded his territory across the major portion of the lands in which his ancestors had been only one of many feuding groups. He seized control of the regions held by the Plantagenet rulers of England. In his enlarged kingdom, Philip created a centralized administration that served to reinforce his rule, and the resulting state became powerful enough to play a major role in European politics.

## The Formation of Normandy

The only region in France that actually gained in status and influence during this period was the duchy of Normandy. Normandy was a relatively recent political creation. In 911 CE, Charles the Simple, king of western Francia, had obtained the assistance of an army of Norsemen (Vikings from Denmark and Norway), in return for which he granted them a coastal region along the English Channel that became the duchy of Normandy. One of the conditions of the treaty was that the Norsemen should convert to Christianity. The Normans, whose name came from the Germanic word *Nortmann*, later became renowned for their energy and fighting prowess as they expelled the Byzantines and Muslims from southern Italy.

## England, Norsemen, and Normandy

Throughout the ninth and early tenth centuries CE, England suffered repeated attacks from Viking invaders. When **Aethelstan** became king in 924 CE, he succeeded in uniting most of the country, and the threat of the Norsemen receded for a while. In 978 CE, Aethelred the Unready became king, and he preferred to pacify the Norsemen by

Edward the Confessor

paying ransoms in gold to prevent further Viking violence. For years, he paid this money (known as **Danegeld**) to buy peace, but in 1002 CE, he organized a large-scale massacre of all the Norsemen in his kingdom to demonstrate his supremacy. The result was disastrous. King Sweyn Forkbeard of Denmark launched his entire fleet to invade England, and a bloody war ensued that lasted until 1013 CE. Finally, exhausted by the continuous fighting, the English accepted Sweyn as king, and Aethelred and his family took refuge in Normandy.

In 1014 CE, Sweyn was succeeded by his son, **Cnut** the Great, who united Denmark, England, and Norway under his rule in 1016 CE. Cnut became a staunch supporter of the church and obtained official recognition from the pope and the emperor as a Christian king. During the eight years of his reign, Cnut was the most powerful ruler in the west, apart from the emperor himself. When Cnut died in 1035 CE, his empire was divided up between his three sons, but when his son Hardecnut died without an heir in 1042 CE, England restored the dynasty of Alfred and Aethelred, bringing the country back under Anglo-Saxon rule.

The new king, Edward (the son of Aethelred the Unready), was so noted for his piety that he became known as Edward the Confessor and was declared a saint by the church in 1161 CE. However, he was a weak king. Edward had been brought up in the ducal court of Normandy and was more at home with the Normans than with the English. Consequently, at his court in England, he surrounded himself with Norman nobles, whom he trusted much more than the rebellious English. England was dominated by powerful men, such Earl Godwin and his son Harold of Wessex, each of whom, in succession, served Edward the Confessor as a kind of prime minister.

Besides the jealousies and rivalries at court, there was an additional problem. Because Edward was unable to produce children, he would die without an heir. There was, however, a surfeit of candidates for the throne. King Harald Hardrade of Norway claimed the right of succession, while Duke **William** of Normandy asserted that Edward had promised him the throne. Harold of Wessex also had his eyes on the throne.

One day in 1064 CE, Harold was sailing on the English Channel when a strong wind drove him onto the coast of Normandy. He was arrested and taken to the court of William of Normandy, where he was cordially received. According to Norman sources, Harold pledged his allegiance to William, an oath that then obliged him to support William's claim to the English throne. However, this story was denied by Harold's supporters.

Harold did help William in a campaign against the Duke of Brittany, an enemy of both the Normans and the English, and later returned to England.

During his final illness, Edward the Confessor named Harold of Wessex as his successor. Harold was crowned the day after the old king died in January of 1066 CE. However, the other claimants to the throne refused to accept Harold of England and mounted separate expeditions to claim the crown of England.

## The Battle of Hastings

Initially, fortune did not favor William of Normandy. A headwind prevented his fleet from setting sail for England. The early leader in the race for the English throne was Harald Hardrade (king of Norway), whose longships crossed the North Sea and landed on the English coast near York. An army of local English lords was waiting for them, but the Norsemen defeated the lords easily. Meanwhile, Harold of England had feverishly mobilized his people's militia and now hurried northward with a scratch army of house carls together with his elite troops. On September 25, 1066 CE, Harold confronted the Norsemen (who were allied with his own brother, Tostig) at Stamford Bridge in Yorkshire. Harold inflicted an overwhelming defeat on the Vikings; Harald Hardrada and Tostig were slain on the field. For the time being at least, Harold's crown was safe.

Almost at once, news reached the English king that the wind in the south had changed and William and his Normans had crossed the channel and landed on the English coast near Hastings on September 28. Harold and his army then marched south, reaching Hastings on October 14.

Harold and his largely untrained soldiers took up position on Senlac Hill, a ridge overlooking the town. William's archers inflicted considerable damage on the tightly packed English army, but the archers, in turn, suffered from the spears and slings directed at them by their adversaries. The Norman cavalry, sent in to attack, was so demoralized by the vicious two-handed battle-axes wielded by the English foot soldiers that it fled from the field.

Although the battle was going badly for the Normans, William rallied his cavalry and made it return to the attack. Then, by pretending to retreat, the invading forces enticed many of the raw English foot soldiers down from their position on the ridge and massacred them. By nightfall, Harold and many of his men were dead, and the few survivors had fled. William made haste to London, where he was crowned king on December 25, 1066 CE.

## A Feudal Nobility

William lost no time in rewarding his Norman supporters. He created some two hundred fiefs and handed them out to his vassals. The vassals, in turn, divided the fiefdoms among their own aids, thereby giving England a new feudal nobility. William was careful, however, to dole out land, not power; the fiefs were small and separated from each other by his own royal preserves. He retained the useful parts of the Anglo-Saxon administrative system, such as the method of tax collection.

The Norman barons set about building stone castles to protect their lands. Such great bastions of power were virtually unknown in pre-Conquest England and were calculated to inspire fear in the Anglo-Saxon population. The native Anglo-Saxons were exploited by the Normans, and it would be more than a century before the two groups adjusted to each other and began to merge into a national culture. The Anglo-Saxon tongue was gradually altered by Norman French and eventually became the English language.

William the Conqueror became one of the most powerful monarchs in Europe. After his death in 1087 CE, England was strongly governed by his sons—first William II Rufus and then Henry I. When Henry I died in 1135 CE, he left only a daughter, Matilda (see box, page 44). After nineteen years of civil war, the crown passed to Matilda's son, Henry Plantagenet (**Henry II**), in 1154 CE.

## Henry II

Henry Plantagenet, duke of Anjou, inherited vast territories in France from his mother, his father, and his brother. Also, through his marriage to **Eleanor of Aquitaine** (the former wife of Louis VII of France), Henry held virtually the whole of southwestern France.

Henry II ruled England and much of France.

Henry II was an energetic ruler who restored order to his troubled realm and brought the English barons to heel. He then reformed the royal administration so that it would continue to function satisfactorily during his frequent absences in France. He gave primary responsibility for all state documents to a chancellor, who became the chief administrator of the kingdom. He also restored and strengthened the office of the exchequer, which administered the country's finances. However, his most impressive accomplishments were in judicial reform.

Henry II simplified the English legal system and created a central court, over which he himself presided. He also introduced traveling justices, who held court in the provinces.

Because Henry owned so much land in France, it became clear that England could no longer remain totally independent. The country was becoming increasingly involved in European affairs. Europe, therefore, had to reckon more seriously with the English king.

## The Domesday Book

Twenty years after William of Normandy conquered England, he set about compiling a survey of his new kingdom. Officials were sent to every county with a brief to document every estate—listing all landholdings and livestock, including every sheep, pig, and goat. The extent of each estate was carefully measured and recorded, together with the number of peasants working on it and any amenities such as fishponds or mills. To ensure that the record was accurate, the king's surveyors made at least two trips to each county.

The survey was completed within two years, and all the information was recorded in two volumes known as the Description of England. By the following century, the survey had become known as the **Domesday Book**, no doubt because there was no appeal against what it recorded, which was used as a basis for levying taxes. Invaluable as it was for William when he needed to raise money for his military ventures, the Domesday Book has been of even greater use to historians by providing a snapshot of England as it was in 1086 CE.

## Louis VII and Eleanor of Aquitaine

In 1137 CE, Louis VII ascended the throne of France. He resembled the English Edward the Confessor both in his piety and in his general incompetence. Fortunately, Louis had many able people at his service, and they succeeded in making their king the most powerful ruler of France to date by arranging a marriage with Eleanor of Aquitaine (fifteen years before her marriage to Henry II), which became the largest fief of the French crown.

## Matilda and Stephen

Matilda (1102–1167 CE) was the daughter of King Henry I of England, and as such, she became an important pawn in the struggle for power in Europe. In 1114 CE, when she was eleven years old, Matilda was married to the Holy Roman emperor Henry V, who died in 1125 CE. Two years later, in 1127 CE, she was married to Geoffrey Plantagenet, count of Anjou, who, at age fifteen, was ten years her junior. Matilda had no children during her first marriage, but with Geoffrey, she had a son, Henry of Anjou, born in 1133 CE. After Henry I's only legitimate son died in 1120 CE, the king named Matilda as his heiress before his own death in 1135 CE.

Matilda should have become queen of England, but the nobles were unwilling to accept a woman as sovereign. Stephen of Blois (Matilda's cousin and a grandson of William the Conqueror) seized the crown with the support of the church and many of the barons. With the help of her half brother, Robert of Gloucester (an illegitimate son of Henry I), Matilda fought for her inheritance. For nineteen years, civil war ravaged England while first one side and then the other seemed to be in the ascendant. At one point, Stephen was defeated and taken prisoner at the Battle of Lincoln, and Matilda entered London with a view to being crowned. However, her perceived arrogance alienated the citizens of London. They rebelled against her, and she was forced to retreat to Oxford. Stephen was later exchanged for Robert of Gloucester, who had been captured by the king's forces. Gradually, Stephen's cause began to prevail.

Matilda fought for her right to the crown for nearly twenty years and became the first woman to rule England.

In 1148 CE, Matilda conceded defeat and withdrew to Normandy. However, peace was not restored to the realm until Matilda's son succeeded Stephen in 1154 CE as Henry II.

The nineteen years of struggle between the forces of Matilda and Stephen were catastrophic for the civilian population. The time became known as Stephen's Anarchy, during which, as one contemporary commentator put it, "Christ and his saints slept."

Matilda was the first female ruler of England. The epitaph on her grave in Rouen, France, is "Here lies the daughter, wife, and mother of Henry."

## Henry II and Thomas Becket: Friendship Turned Foul

When Henry II became king of England in 1154 CE, he was determined to reestablish strong central government in a country that had been torn apart by years of civil war. He found a loyal ally in **Thomas Becket**, his chancellor.

Henry relied heavily on Becket. In 1162 CE, hoping to gain support from the church, the king made Becket archbishop of Canterbury. It proved to be a fatal miscalculation. In the same dedicated fashion with which he had once worked for the king, Becket now began to serve the interests of the church, and the two old friends became bitter enemies.

Their most intense conflict erupted over the English system of jurisdiction. Henry sought absolute control over church as well as state jurisdiction. In the Clarendon Constitution, he asserted that clerics (who were normally tried by the church) should in the future be tried by royal authorities. Any appeal to the pope would be allowed only with royal consent.

Becket opposed Henry's attempt to undermine church law. He quarreled with the king and then went into exile in France, where he remained for six years. From France, Becket continued to write pamphlets condemning Henry's activities. Although the pope agreed in principle with Becket, he did not wish to antagonize the king, so he remained on the sidelines.

Fresh controversy arose in 1170 CE, when Henry asked the archbishop of York to crown his son. Becket fired off an angry letter, excommunicating Henry. Henry, worried that the pope might put an interdict on the whole of England, visited Becket in France. An agreement was patched up, and Becket returned to Canterbury. However, four of Henry's vassals overheard the king wondering aloud if nobody could free him of this irritating cleric. They took his words literally, and on December 29, 1170 CE, they forced their way into Canterbury Cathedral and slew Becket in front of the altar.

The fact that the marriage ended in disaster was not the fault of the advisors but of the spouses. Eleanor and Louis hated each other almost on sight. Louis was dull and sheepish, while Eleanor was lively and spirited. After fifteen miserable years, Louis wanted to divorce his wife; he was willing to give up Aquitaine in exchange for his happiness. The marriage was annulled, officially because a close genetic relationship was said to exist between the king and his wife, but unofficially because Eleanor had failed to give the king a son.

Eleanor was furious about the humiliation she had suffered. She married again almost immediately in 1152 CE, this time to Henry Plantagenet, duke of Anjou (two years before he became king of England). Henry had already succeeded to the duchy of Normandy, and the addition of Eleanor's fief of Aquitaine made Henry by far the most powerful man in France.

Louis responded by conspiring with his remaining vassals against Henry. Consequently, Henry had to face constant resistance in his French lands. Only in England did he succeed in installing a durable system of government.

## Philip II Augustus Regains France

In 1180 CE, Louis VII died and was succeeded by Philip Augustus, his son by Adèle of Champagne. Aged fifteen on his accession, Philip did not cut an impressive figure. He was weak and sickly and at first showed little interest in fighting battles. He did, however, prove himself an accomplished diplomat, with a talent for intrigue. In the early years of his reign, he set about extending his territories by marriage. The duchy of Artois in northern France came to him as a dowry when he married Isabella of Hainault.

By winning a war with local princes, he gained power over Vermandois (a region to the northeast of Paris), so that Eleanor of Aquitaine, who was also countess of Vermandois, had to swear allegiance to him.

Meanwhile, disorder broke out in England as Henry II's sons—Henry, Geoffrey, Richard, and John—fought over their inheritance. Philip used intrigue whenever he could to fan the flames, ultimately supporting John and Richard in a conspiracy against their father. The old king was eventually forced to back down and died shortly afterward.

Eleanor of Aquitaine convinced her son Richard I to pardon his brother Prince John.

His two older brothers having died, **Richard I** (Richard the Lionheart; see sidebar, page 51) succeeded Henry. Although John was granted considerable estates, bringing him an income of £6,000 a year, he was not satisfied with his situation, and Philip provided assistance to him behind the scenes. The result was a protracted war between Richard and Philip, and John played a devious role in this war.

In 1199 CE, Richard died during a siege and was succeeded by John. To further his own interests, Philip needed to look for another contender to the English throne, and he chose John's nephew Arthur, the young Duke of Brittany. A state of war soon existed between John and Philip, and John was gradually put on the defensive by Philip's military and diplomatic machinations. After several years of fighting, John was finally forced to cede all but one of his French possessions to Philip; the sole remaining English territory in France was the duchy of Gascony.

Philip was now the king of almost all of France, and he took advantage of the feudal system to consolidate his rule and outwit his opponents. For example, in 1200 CE, John had married Isabella of Angoulême, partly with a view to gaining the territory in France to which his bride was heiress. However, Isabella was already betrothed to the count of La Marche. The breaking of the betrothal entitled the jilted party to compensation, and the count appealed for it to the French king in Paris. Philip summoned John, who was formally still his vassal, to appear before the vassal court. As expected, John refused to appear, and Philip, as his lord, declared John's fiefs annulled. In practice, this declaration had to be enforced by military means, but the principle of the king as supreme lord was confirmed.

Also at this time, the Holy Roman Empire was being torn apart by a civil war between pretenders to the throne. Philip and John supported rival claimants in their continuing efforts to promote their own interests and thwart each other's ambitions. In 1214, John and Holy Roman Emperor Otto IV mounted a two-pronged attack on their common enemy. Suddenly, Philip was threatened on both his eastern and western flanks. After consulting his advisors, Philip decided to deal with Otto first.

Leaving only eight hundred knights to guard his western border, which was threatened by the English, Philip ordered his main army to await the entrance into France of Otto's forces. When the armies engaged near the town of Bouvines, Otto suffered a major defeat and John's forces withdrew. The citizens of Paris celebrated for several days, and Philip made a triumphal return to the city. His throne and his kingdom were both saved. By his victory, Philip had strengthened his hold on most of the former English possessions in France.

Philip Augustus, King of France

Philip's military successes left him free to strengthen his administrative grip on France. In doing so, he deliberately moved away from the old feudal structures and created a new position, that of the bailiff. The bailiff was not a vassal; he was a salaried official whose job was to administer a district of the kingdom according to directives from Paris. Bailiffs reported annually to Paris, and they could be transferred to other districts, thereby ensuring that they did not become too entrenched in one region. Consequently, bailiffs were completely dependent on the monarch for position and income. In this way, Philip created an administrative system whose officials were likely to be loyal to the king.

## Absolute Monarchies

By 1200, the kings of France and England had similar powers, but they had acquired them by quite different means. In England, William I's conquest had converted the realm at one fell swoop into an absolute monarchy, albeit one in which the monarch pulled as many feudal strings as possible. In France, the development of absolute monarchy was more gradual. The Capets maintained a low profile for generations, paying minimal attention to the kingdom as a whole, while they strengthened their grip on their own core territory. In the twelfth century, during the feudal struggle with their most powerful vassal, Henry Plantagenet, the French kings established undisputed authority. Having achieved that, they developed an administrative system independent of their vassals, using officials whom they controlled because they were employees.

## Richard the Lionheart

Richard the Lionheart (ruled 1189–1199 CE) was one of the most colorful and charismatic kings of England, yet he spent barely six months of his reign in his kingdom. The third son of Henry II, Richard had been raised at the court of his mother, Eleanor, in Aquitaine, where he became skilled in knightly combat. When he inherited the English throne, his first thought was that this would allow him to fulfill his ambition to lead a crusade and retake Jerusalem, which had been captured in 1187 CE by the Muslim leader Saladin. After raising as much money as he could from his new kingdom, Richard assembled an army and a fleet and set sail for the Holy Land.

The crusaders captured Acre in 1191 CE, and Richard won a great victory over Saladin at the Battle of Arsuf. He then came within sight of Jerusalem but could not take the city. The allies quarreled among themselves, and Richard had to be content with a three-year truce with Saladin. Under the truce, Christian pilgrims were allowed to visit the holy places.

Hearing that his brother, John, was conspiring with the king of France, Richard sailed for home. He was shipwrecked near Venice and captured by Duke Leopold of Austria, who handed him over to Holy Roman Emperor Henry VI. Henry kept Richard imprisoned for four years, releasing him only on the promise of a ransom. Richard's time in captivity gave rise to the legend that the French troubadour Blondel discovered where the king was held by singing the first verse of a song outside the prison walls and hearing Richard sing the second verse.

Released from prison, Richard returned briefly to England and then went to Normandy, where he spent the last five years of his life in constant battles against Philip Augustus. Laying siege to the castle of Chalus in 1199 CE, Richard was hit by an arrow from a lone crossbow archer and died a few days later.

Richard was an outstanding soldier, an accomplished politician, and a poet of renown. Yet, in England, he is remembered chiefly as a relentless collector of taxes to fuel his military exploits and to pay the exorbitant ransom demanded for him by the Holy Roman emperor.

Barbarossa, also known as Frederick I, with his two sons Henry VI and Duke Frederick

CHAPTER FOUR

# Emperors and Popes

In Europe, the second half of the twelfth century was dominated by renewed conflict between the papacy and the Holy Roman Empire. At the start of the thirteenth century CE, church and state found common purpose in the **Fourth Crusade**.

In the twelfth century, the Holy Roman emperor was elected by the rulers of Germany's principalities and duchies who, together with the leading bishops, each had a vote in selecting the new emperor. After the German emperor Henry V died in 1125 CE, that procedure caused a civil war. One faction of nobles wanted a strong emperor who would base his power on the church; that faction chose Conrad of the house of Hohenstaufen as its candidate. The other faction was a reforming party that supported the pope against the emperor; the pope did not want emperors to appoint bishops, and neither did he want his papal vassals to further their own interests. The second faction supported Lothair, a member of the Welf family, and it was he who was elected king and crowned as Holy Roman Emperor Lothair II by Pope Innocent II in 1133 CE.

The rivalry over the imperial succession started years of dynastic feuding. The Hohenstaufen supporters were called Waiblingen, after a favorite castle of the Hohenstaufen dukes of Swabia. The other party called itself the Welfs, after the Welf dynasty of Bavaria. The struggle spilled over into Italy, where the warring factions called themselves **Ghibellines** (Waiblingen) and **Guelphs** (Welfs).

After twenty-seven years of confusion and strife, a compromise appeared to have been reached in 1152 CE, when the rulers of Germany elected Frederick of Hohenstaufen as their king. Frederick's mother was a Welf, and because he was descended from both **Hohenstaufens** and Welfs, it was hoped that he would put an end to discord in the kingdom. Frederick was nicknamed Barbarossa (*barba* meaning "beard" and *rossa* meaning "red") because of his facial hair.

On his accession, Frederick was faced with the seemingly impossible task of restoring the authority of the emperor after it had been seriously eroded by the outcome of the controversy over lay **investiture**—the right of temporal rulers (kings, counts, dukes, and so on) to appoint spiritual officials (bishops, priests, and so on). That issue had been of special concern to Pope Gregory VII (ruled 1073–1085 CE). Gregory had tried to end the practice by which royalty could "invest" bishops—giving them the ring and staff that were the symbols of their office. Because bishops often held secular positions (which made them vassals of the king) as well as their church appointments, lay investiture seemed reasonable under feudalism. However, at the **Concordat of Worms** in 1122 CE, the church had been granted the right to elect and invest new bishops. The emperor was to be present at the ceremony, where he would confer any property of the bishopric on the new bishop, using a nonreligious symbol, the scepter. The resolution at Worms enhanced the clerics' administrative authority but undermined Frederick's.

Frederick had another problem. A large part of his realm had been granted in fief to his supporters in order to secure their loyalty in the fight over the succession to the throne. The royal vassals who had been granted fiefdoms had given them, in turn, to minor nobles, who arranged for serfs to work the land. That was the beginning of feudalization in the German Empire. Under this system, each duke controlled a duchy of his own, and as a result, many of the dukes were in very strong positions. Some of them had even more power than the emperor.

## Barbarossa Invades Italy

Imperial authority was also challenged by the great cities that had grown up in the Italian part of the empire. The merchant aristocracies of those cities had taken over the control that had once been held by the resident bishops and the emperor. Frederick turned his attention to Italy, hoping that an Italian adventure might divert the attention of his barons from the fragile balance of power at home. As had happened so often in the past, the state of affairs in Rome provided the justification for his intervention.

Coronation of Frederick I

The majority of Romans at that time refused to accept the political sovereignty of the pope and had established a council of citizens, called the commune, to which the pope was required to submit. Several popes were forced into exile for denying the authority of the commune, and street fights over the issue were a regular occurrence. Pope Hadrian IV (ruled 1154–1159 CE) faced a particularly virulent uprising and realized that he needed Frederick's help in suppressing the communal movement.

Frederick crossed the Alps in 1154–1155 CE and advanced quickly to Rome, where he was crowned Holy Roman emperor by Hadrian. However, a point of contention soon arose. It was a custom at the time for the ruler of the Holy Roman Empire to hold the pope's stirrup as a sign of homage when he wished to dismount from his mule. Frederick objected to making such a gesture of subservience. As he hesitated, the pope arrogantly commanded him to hold the stirrup. Frederick did so, but was heard to say: "For Petrus [Saint Peter], not for Hadrian."

Another incident took place two years later. During a meeting of the Diet (the German parliament) held in Besançon in 1157 CE, a letter arrived from the pope. It contained the following sentence:

"It would have pleased the pope if, in addition to the emperor's crown, Your Excellency had also received from our hands even larger *beneficia*."

The word beneficia had two meanings. Originally, it had meant "benediction" or "blessing," but in official documents, it was used to mean "fiefdom." The implication was clear—that the pope had the right to grant lands to the emperor. The Diet was furious, and Cardinal Roland, the messenger, was nearly stoned. Frederick declared that he took his power only "from God," not from the pope.

## Italy Rebels

A year after the Besançon incident, the emperor crossed the Alps again, determined to impose his imperial authority on the largely independent cities of Lombardy. During a Diet session in Roncaglia, Frederick demanded the restoration of royal prerogatives, including the collection of tolls and taxes and the minting of coins, all of which had traditionally been matters for the government but had long ago fallen into the hands of local rulers. To enforce his demands, Frederick sent podestas (hired strong men) to every city in Lombardy.

It was a gamble. The Italian cities united against the podestas, and Frederick was suddenly faced with a dangerous rebellion. To quell the insurgents, the emperor first laid siege to Milan, the center of the rebellion. It took several years to subdue the city, which he then razed to the ground in 1162 CE, driving out the inhabitants in the process. The fate of Milan was enough to make the other cities proceed more cautiously.

In the meantime, Pope Hadrian had died, and the assembled cardinals elected Cardinal Roland as his successor. As Pope Alexander III (ruled 1159–1181 CE), the former cardinal became Frederick's most dangerous opponent. The voting session had been divided, however, and one faction elected a rival pope, Victor IV, who became in effect an antipope. Victor had Frederick's support, and despite the fact that he was recognized only in areas under Frederick's control, Victor's influence was such that Alexander was forced to vacate Rome and flee to France.

At the same time, it became apparent that Frederick's earlier victory in Italy was far from definitive. In 1167 CE, a union of northern Italian cities, known as the **Lombard League**, was formed with the active support of Pope Alexander to oppose the authority of the emperor. After some delay, Frederick invaded Italy yet again, but he was defeated by the forces of the Lombard League at the Battle of Legnano in 1176 CE.

In the wake of his defeat, Frederick was forced to come to terms with the pope. The terms demanded by Alexander were moderate. The antipope had to step down, and Alexander had to be recognized, but Frederick was allowed to retain his sovereignty over the German church. Frederick also concluded a peace treaty with the Lombard League, based on a compromise. He ceded most of his imperial rights in the cities in exchange for the recognition of his authority by the urban magistrates. All new appointments would be subject to confirmation by the emperor.

## Increasing Frederick's Reach in Germany

Frederick now turned his attention to the German part of his empire. The barons watched anxiously as he tried to reduce his dependency on them by modifying the feudal system that had given them so much power.

By the twelfth century, common people could rise fairly high in the imperial court as civil servants known as *ministeriales*. Frederick made the ministeriales the foundation of his rule by putting them in charge of large territories. He also won the loyalty of the minor nobles by giving them choice positions at court, which they vastly preferred to tending their small estates in the country. The church felt Frederick's hand also because he kept control over church appointments.

Such methods ran counter to the Welf concept of imperial rule and aroused the ire of the Welf dukes. The most powerful of them was the duke of Saxony, Henry the Lion (1129–1195 CE), who had ambitions to wear the imperial crown himself. Henry had refused to participate in Frederick's most recent Italian campaign, and after the emperor's defeat at the Battle of Legnano, Henry openly opposed him.

Frederick realized that he had to get rid of Henry. Complaints from Henry's fiefdom provided the excuse for Frederick to summon Henry before a royal court of justice. However, the Saxon duke refused to attend. Using arguments from regional, feudal, and even Roman law, the emperor convinced a council of princes to depose Henry, after which the duke's vast lands were divided up among Frederick's supporters. As a result, the emperor's power increased dramatically.

Italy was still in the forefront of Frederick's mind. He arranged a marriage between his oldest son, Henry, and Constance, heiress to the Norman kingdom of Sicily. Through this union, the powerful nation of Sicily—once the emperor's sworn enemy and a devoted supporter of the pope—came into Hohenstaufen hands.

## Frederick Dies

In 1189 CE, Pope Clement III (ruled 1187–1191 CE) found himself in a quandary. When almost all of western Christendom was preparing for the **Third Crusade**, the only leader on whom the pope could call for support was Frederick I. Although the emperor joined the crusade, he missed his chance at immortality (which the crusaders were promised) by drowning in a river on his way to Turkey in 1190 CE.

However, Frederick did become a legend in Germany in the sixteenth to eighteenth centuries. He sleeps in a mountain, it was said, and if you put your ear to a certain stone, you can hear his beard grow. It was believed that he would only reawaken when Germany was in very great danger.

After the death of Frederick, the Hohenstaufen triumphs continued. Frederick's son, the emperor Henry VI, was accorded imperial recognition, not only in Germany but also in Italy. Through his wife, Henry VI controlled the Norman kingdom of Sicily, the best-organized state in Christendom.

The widespread recognition of Henry aroused the opposition of the pope. Blocked by the emperor at every turn, the pope saw the traditional papal support of the Normans disappear and his own position in the Papal States threatened. Yet, twenty years after Frederick Barbarossa's death, the papacy reached the pinnacle of its power, during the reign of Innocent III (1198–1216 CE).

## *Dominium Mundi*

The controversy over lay investiture had made many people reconsider the place of the Church within the political system. If the pope was indeed the representative of Christ on earth, they asked, how could he have superiors? Even the emperor must be considered to be below the pope, a position implicit in the fact that the emperor received his crown from the hands of the pope. In this view, it was argued, the pope possessed *dominium mundi* (sovereignty over the world), which implied that he had supervisory responsibility for the actions of all secular rulers.

In reality, there was little to substantiate that claim in the first half of the twelfth century. The popes were not allowed to govern even in their own city, let alone to achieve dominium mundi. The papacy attracted attention outside Rome only when the pope required allies against the emperor.

When Henry VI came to the throne, the pope found himself even more threatened. Henry was a bold man who did not look kindly on half measures. He achieved his goals through warfare; although he was nominally king of Sicily, he had to go to war to take control of the island, which he finally achieved in 1194 CE. He then attacked the Lombard cities, and his victories over them also gave him control over an important part of the Papal States. The pope now found himself surrounded on all sides by an increasingly aggressive emperor who frequently spoke of his ambition to dominate the whole world.

However, Henry VI died of malaria in 1197 CE, leaving a three-year-old son, **Frederick II**, as emperor. Seizing the opportunity, the Welf faction set up its own claimant to the throne—Otto of Brunswick, the son of Henry the Lion of Saxony. Because Frederick was too young to fight for his crown, his cause was taken up by his uncle, Philip of Swabia, and war broke out between the two sides.

## Papal Supremacy and Pope Innocent III

Innocent III became pope in 1198 CE. He was well educated, particularly in theology and canon law, and he was extremely ambitious. He came from a powerful Roman family, and he was ordained a cardinal deacon and played an active role in the government of the Vatican when his kinsman Celestine III was pope.

After Innocent became pope, he was determined to restore papal supremacy. He first reconciled his differences with the old enemy of papal authority, the city council of Rome, by withdrawing altogether from the city government. Turning to the rest of the country,

Pope Innocent III

Innocent subjugated the troublesome nobles of the Papal States with cold-blooded violence.

With nothing now to fear at home, Innocent looked to the war raging in Germany between the rival claimants to the imperial crown. He chose to support the Welf Otto of Brunswick against Philip of Swabia, and Otto IV was duly crowned emperor in 1209, after promising to give up all attempts to influence church appointments.

In the south, Innocent sided with the Hohenstaufens against the Sicilian nobles. He assisted the widow of Henry VI in getting her son, Frederick, recognized as heir to the Sicilian throne. However, the price of papal support was high. The sovereignty the Sicilian rulers had always enjoyed over the church passed into the hands of the pope, and Henry's widow had to swear fealty to Innocent. She also appointed the pope as guardian to the child.

Innocent then found that his trust in Otto had been misplaced. After his coronation as emperor, Otto reneged on his promises, meddled in church appointments, and launched an invasion of Sicily. In 1210, Innocent excommunicated Otto and proposed to place Frederick on the throne. Otto allied himself with John of England (who, like himself, was an enemy of Philip II Augustus of France), but at the Battle of Bouvines in 1214, Otto was defeated by Philip. Otto then gave up his dreams of empire and retired to his Brunswick estates.

Frederick II was finally elected emperor in 1215, eighteen years after he inherited the title from his father, but major concessions were demanded by the pope. Frederick had to repeat all of Otto's promises and swear that he would never unite Sicily with the Holy Roman Empire.

## Papal Punishment

Although Philip II Augustus of France had been instrumental in clearing the way for Innocent's protégé to become the Holy Roman emperor, his relations with Innocent were stormy. The pope even put France under an interdict—a papal punishment that meant no sacraments could take place in the country. For medieval Christians, this was a severe punishment that barred the path to salvation.

The move was in response to Philip's treatment of his second wife. After the death of his first wife, Isabella of Hainault, in 1189 CE, the French king married again in 1193 CE. His new consort was a Danish princess, Ingebord. Through her, Philip formed an alliance with Cnut IV of Denmark, which was still a relatively important power. The marriage was performed with great ceremony, and after the festivities, the bride and groom retired for their wedding night. However, the next morning Philip banned his wife from the palace. The reason was never disclosed, but the unhappy bride retired to a convent, where she spent the next twenty years. As a final insult, Philip had the marriage annulled by a council of bishops.

Ingebord appealed to the pope, who countermanded her husband's repudiation. When Philip persisted in his refusal to take Ingebord back, Innocent proclaimed the interdict. However, the interdict was not obeyed in most of Philip's domains. On the whole, religious life in France continued as usual.

In 1196 CE, Philip married Agnes of Meran, who bore him two children. That marriage was not recognized by the pope, but after Agnes's death in 1201, a compromise was reached. Philip took Ingebord back in 1213, and the pope recognized the legitimacy of the French king's children with Agnes.

## England and the Magna Carta

King John of England, Philip's longtime adversary, also had a troubled relationship with Innocent. In 1207, the pope appointed Stephen

## The Fourth Crusade

Saladin and his Saracens captured Jerusalem in 1187 CE, and it was one of Pope Innocent III's greatest ambitions to see the Holy City recaptured from the Muslims.

In 1202, Innocent was instrumental in raising a new army of crusaders. The plan was to sail from Venice to the Holy Land, but departure was delayed while the crusaders sought sponsors. Eventually, an agreement was reached with the Venetian merchants, whereby the merchants agreed to finance the expedition if, in return, the crusaders would help to recapture the Venetian satellite city of Zara.

Within a week, Zara had fallen, but the pope, incensed by this use of his crusading army, excommunicated the whole expedition. The crusaders then set out for Constantinople, where they planned to depose the usurping Byzantine emperor, Alexius III, and enthrone another Alexius, the son of Isaac Angelus (the legitimate emperor, who was old and blind). The incentive for this action was a promise by the young Alexius to finance a conquest of Egypt and bring the church of Constantinople back under the authority of the pope in Rome.

This part of the expedition was a huge success—for the crusaders. Constantinople was captured, burned, and plundered in 1204, but while the young Alexius was briefly crowned emperor along with his father, he was soon murdered by a nobleman named Murzuphlus, who was then crowned Alexius V. The crusaders reassembled and attacked Constantinople for a second time, replacing Alexius V with one of their own leaders, Baldwin, count of Flanders.

As the main victor, Venice was rewarded with vast tracts of land and the right to trade freely throughout the Byzantine Empire.

*The Taking of Constantinople*, painted by Domenico Tintoretto

Hundreds of crusaders became the Byzantine emperor's vassals and received grants of land, although they often had to conquer the lands themselves. The rest of the army went home with gold, works of art, and precious manuscripts. The Fourth Crusade never reached Jerusalem, and Innocent's dream of recapturing the city was never realized.

The Latin Empire of Constantinople was torn apart by internal divisions and lasted for less than sixty years. In a few parts of the empire, however, the Greek sovereigns remained in power, and in 1261, one of them, Michael Paleologus, king of Nicaea, reconquered Constantinople.

Magna Carta, or Great Charter, which is currently displayed in the British Library. The seal has been lost to time, but the parchment is still in good condition.

Langton as the archbishop of Canterbury, but John refused to allow the new archbishop into the country. Innocent retaliated by placing England under an interdict and excommunicating the king.

The situation dragged on until 1212, when John was forced to accept Langton's appointment because he needed the pope's assistance in his disputes with his vassals. John even agreed to become a vassal of the pope—in effect, officially recognizing the doctrine of dominium mundi. Once the oath of fealty had been sworn, Innocent wholeheartedly supported his new vassal.

The English barons were becoming increasingly disgruntled by John's heavy taxes to finance his efforts to reclaim his lost lands in France. After John withdrew from France following the Battle of Bouvines in 1214, the barons threatened rebellion. John was presented with a list of demands that set out a grant of English liberties covering the rights of the church, the feudal barons, and the cities. Crucially, the document stated that the king was not allowed to impose taxes without his vassals' consent. A council of twenty-five barons was appointed to monitor the king's compliance with the document and given the right to go to war against him if he failed to abide by it.

The document was finalized with the assistance of Stephen Langton and sealed by John at Runnymede on the banks of the Thames River in the presence of his barons on June 15, 1215. The document was called **Magna Carta** (Great Charter).

Even as copies of the charter were being sent throughout the kingdom, John regretted his capitulation. He appealed to his liege lord, Innocent III, and the pope promptly rescinded the entire charter because, in his opinion, it ran counter to the law and the rights of kings. That action threatened to provoke civil war in England, but John died in 1216, and when his infant son, Henry III, came to the throne, the king's councilors reinstated the charter.

## A Shameful Crusade

When Innocent III died in 1216, he was at the height of his power. He had played an active part in the politics of Europe, and in some cases, he had succeeded in turning his spiritual sovereignty into political sovereignty by insisting that lay rulers swear fealty to him. The pope had also been largely responsible for the launch of the Fourth Crusade. Unfortunately, however, the crusade never reached the Holy Land; it degenerated into the sacking of Constantinople, with the crusaders devastating the city and carrying off many of its treasures. Although the pope excommunicated the perpetrators of this outrage, it is not clear how sincerely he opposed the subjugation of Constantinople. It may be that he hoped it would result in a reunification of the western and eastern churches, which had been divided since the Great Schism of 1054 CE.

Nevertheless, Innocent III never stopped dreaming of liberating Jerusalem from the Muslims. Less than a year before his death, the pope made his ward, Frederick II, promise to lead another crusade. The young emperor would later fulfill this promise, but in a very different way from anything that Innocent might have imagined.

Frederick II, Holy Roman Emperor

CHAPTER FIVE

# Monarchs of the Middle Ages

Between 1200 and 1300, the kings of Europe faced numerous challenges from the church, and some of them became involved in military adventures in the Holy Land. They also had to contend with the growing power of their noblemen.

Frederick of Hohenstaufen was only twenty years old when he became Holy Roman Emperor Frederick II in 1215. Heir to the throne of both the Sicilian kingdom and the Holy Roman Empire, Frederick had been brought up in Sicily, where he was surrounded by court intrigue. In his youth, he had wandered through the multilingual metropolis of Palermo, loitering around the harbor, visiting synagogues and mosques, and bombarding passersby with a multitude of questions. This daily contact with the city's diverse population gave him a vast general knowledge and fluency in both Arabic and Greek.

Frederick was mercurial; he could be charming one minute and hostile the next. He had an independent and inquiring mind. He made his own assessment of everyone and everything, and he became a scholar with an encyclopedic grasp of facts. He was familiar with the teachings of the Prophet Mohammed, as well as with those of Moses and Jesus, and he liked to suggest that he had not discovered the truth in any of them.

Frederick enjoyed a good relationship with Muslims; they provided his court with scholars, manuscripts, Oriental rugs, and most of the animals that made up his famous menagerie. Frederick became an expert in falconry and wrote a guide to the art.

## A Wonder of the World

A mystery to most of his subjects, Frederick became known as *stupor mundi* (wonder of the world). He set out to continue the policies of his father and grandfather. Realizing that the power of the Hohenstaufen family had been dangerously undermined north of the Alps, he concentrated his powerbase in Italy. He signed an agreement with his German nobles that allowed them to handle their own affairs, and then he left them largely to their own devices.

The system worked well. After concluding this agreement, Frederick made only one further visit to Germany, when one of his own sons rebelled. This son, Henry, had been left in Germany as his father's representative and was elected king of Germany in 1220. In 1234, Henry formed an alliance with the Lombard League and led a revolt against his father. However, the rebels surrendered as soon as Frederick arrived in Germany the following year. Henry was captured, deposed, and transported to Italy, where he would have been imprisoned had he not taken the opportunity en route to jump to his death in a ravine.

In Italy, Frederick II aimed to achieve complete domination of the entire peninsula. In his Sicilian kingdom, he established an absolute monarchy and dealt harshly with opponents, having them routinely blinded, castrated, and burned alive. Frederick turned his Sicilian kingdom into the most modern state in the west.

A well-oiled official machine governed the state according to the emperor's wishes. Frederick raised money through progressive taxation, a system that makes the rich people pay more taxes than the poor people do. Although this system of taxation appeared equitable, Frederick's subjects paid the highest taxes in the world. That his people were also the most prosperous and the best protected cut little ice with them. The "wonder of the world" was widely regarded as a tyrant.

## The Papacy and Frederick II

Frederick II enjoyed cordial relations with Pope Honorius III. The emperor even restored papal authority in central Italy, where local

Frederick II meets with the sultan to negotiate a treaty.

leaders had regained power after the death of Innocent III in 1216. However, Frederick failed to fulfill his promise to Innocent III about going on a crusade.

In 1227, Honorius III died and was succeeded by Gregory IX. The new pope immediately threatened Frederick with excommunication if he refused to launch a crusade. Frederick accordingly equipped and sent out a fleet, but an epidemic broke out among the crews and the ships were forced to turn back. Gregory refused to accept Frederick's excuses and excommunicated him.

The following year, Frederick organized another crusade. He had, in the meantime, married Isabella, who was heiress to the kingdom of Jerusalem. In addition, the emperor had been carrying on clandestine negotiations with the sultan of Egypt, who, alarmed by the advance of the army of the Fifth Crusade, signed a treaty that gave Jerusalem to Frederick in exchange for certain guarantees for the indigenous Muslims. In 1229, Frederick made a peaceful entrance into the Holy City, where he was crowned king. Gregory was not pleased; crusaders were meant to win wars, not negotiate with infidels.

Frederick returned to Sicily without delay after the coronation ceremony. He installed his queen in the palace and thereafter paid little or no attention to her; he had decided to assert his claims to the rest of Italy. However, he had to reckon with the pope and the Lombard League because both the papacy and the independent cities had good reason to resist Frederick's domination.

The ensuing war lasted for twenty years. On the whole, luck was with the emperor; at one point, Innocent IV, who succeeded Gregory IX in 1243, even had to flee to France. In 1245, the pope tried unsuccessfully to organize a crusade against the excommunicated emperor. Five years later, Frederick died just when he seemed to have gained the upper hand in the conflict.

## The Hohenstaufens End

Frederick's successor, Conrad IV, had been installed in Germany as Frederick's deputy in 1235. As soon as Conrad heard of his father Frederick's death in 1250, he crossed the Alps to take over his Italian inheritance but found that his powerbase had been seriously undermined; most of northern Italy had fallen back into the hands of the pope. When Conrad died in 1254, his son, Conradin, was still a child. Conrad's half-brother, Manfred, took over the leadership in Italy, while Conradin stayed on in Germany.

The Sicilian kingdom was all that remained for Manfred to rule, and it was not until 1258 that Manfred was able to become a real threat to the pope and the Lombard cities. By then, however, the entire house of Hohenstaufen had been excommunicated.

In 1263, the pope granted the crown of the Sicilian kingdom to Charles of Anjou, the younger brother of the French king Louis IV. To win his kingdom, Charles fought Manfred at the Battle of Benevento in 1266. Manfred was killed, leaving Charles as king of Sicily. Charles then moved to consolidate his power throughout the Sicilian kingdom, beating back any and all Ghibelline resistance. In this process of consolidation, the Ghibelline champion, the young Conradin, was captured and beheaded in Palermo market in front of a great crowd; the last member of the Hohenstaufen dynasty came to an inglorious end.

## The Sicilian Vespers

Charles's victory brought many French immigrants into the Sicilian kingdom. Many of the newcomers became government officials, ruthlessly extorting money to finance the creation of an empire that embraced the entire Mediterranean. Charles and his administration became universally hated. Although the Sicilians paid the money that was demanded of them, anti-French feeling intensified.

At the hour of vespers on Easter Monday in 1282, a crowd gathered outside Palermo's city gate. The people had been celebrating the holiday, and a dispute arose between a young husband and an intoxicated

The Sicilian Vespers was a conflict that was fueled by tensions between Sicilians and the new French immigrants. It ended in a bloody riot.

Frenchman who, the Sicilians claimed, had been showing too much interest in the man's wife. The husband, offended and probably not too sober himself, attacked the Frenchman. A fight broke out. When the Frenchman collapsed, stabbed with a dagger, his fellow countrymen rushed into the fray to help him. The Sicilians' hatred of the French boiled over, and that night, more than two thousand French inhabitants of Palermo were murdered in a massacre that became known as the **Sicilian Vespers**. Charles was forced to retreat to Naples.

The Sicilians rose in revolt and offered their kingdom to Peter III of Aragon (who was married to a daughter of Manfred). A long, indecisive war ensued. After several years, Charles was forced to accept the situation. He had to content himself with southern Italy, which he ruled from Naples, while the kings of Aragon retained Sicily.

The situation pleased many people but not Charles himself. His former empire was divided and could no longer challenge the Lombard cities or the papacy. One consequence of these developments was that the papacy became stronger politically, but these gains were more than offset by a simultaneous decline in the pope's appeal as a spiritual leader.

## Simon de Montfort

Simon de Montfort was born in France around 1208. On coming of age, he renounced his French inheritance and claimed the English earldom of Leicester, to which he was entitled through his paternal grandmother.

Simon de Montfort and the Battle of Evesham

Simon de Montfort traveled to England in 1229 and paid homage to Henry III. He became a great favorite of the king, married the king's sister Eleanor in 1238, and was finally granted the title Earl of Leicester in 1239. He established his headquarters at Kenilworth Castle in Warwickshire. However, de Montfort's relationship with the king deteriorated during the next twenty years. In 1258, he and other discontented barons, convinced that Henry was no longer fit to rule, demanded concessions, known as the Provisions of Oxford. The Provisions stipulated that a parliament should meet three times a year and that there should be a permanent council to advise the king.

The king agreed to these conditions at first but soon reneged on his promises. De Montfort defeated royal forces at the Battle of Lewes in 1264, taking both Henry and his son, Edward, prisoner. For the next fifteen months, de Montfort ruled England in the king's name, summoning parliaments that included knights and burgesses as well as nobles.

However, some barons remained loyal to the king, and they helped Edward to escape from prison in Hereford Castle. Edward assembled a new army and, in August of 1265, confronted de Montfort at the Battle of Evesham. The bulk of the rebels had already been routed by a royalist force near their base at Kenilworth, and now their remaining forces were defeated. De Montfort himself was killed, and his head was exhibited on a pike on the walls of Evesham Castle as a warning to all traitors.

The idea of dominium mundi (sovereignty over the world) was at last losing ground.

## English Rebellion

Under Henry II, England had seemed on its way to becoming the best organized monarchy in Western Europe, but the behavior of his sons, Richard I (the Lionheart) and John, had reversed this trend. The continual bickering over feudal estates in France had weakened royal power, and the English kings spent much time and money trying to reconquer the disputed areas. One result of this was the growth of the political power of the barons at home.

Rather than attempting to undermine the monarchy, the barons sought a role in government. Their demands, reflected in Magna Carta (1215), became more imperative later in the century. The barons fought against Henry III (ruled 1216–1272), and their confrontation came to a head in 1264, when a rebellion, led by Simon de Montfort, Earl of Leicester, defeated the royal forces and captured the king. De Montfort's success was short-lived. Fifteen months later, Henry's son, Edward, defeated the rebels and restored his father to the throne. However, Henry was in his dotage by this time, and Edward ruled in his name, becoming Edward I on Henry's death in 1272.

## The Rule of Edward I

Edward I (ruled 1272–1307) continued his father's efforts to regain the power of the central monarchy. He was an energetic warrior who, like his forebears, was keenly interested in territorial expansion. He targeted Wales, Ireland, and Scotland.

Edward succeeded in permanently subduing the whole of Wales, where he built a series of castles to keep the local population under control. To mark his success in the country, he made his son the Prince of Wales—a title that has since been held by the eldest son of every English monarch. In Scotland, Edward was less successful; his invading armies laid the country to waste, but he was heroically resisted by the Scottish king, Robert the Bruce, and the struggle strengthened the determination of the Scots to remain independent. Edward also fought with France to protect his duchy of Gascony.

An important feature of Edward I's reign was the king's willingness to convene parliaments, a practice that had been started by his father. These parliaments were councils that consisted not only of royal vassals but also of representatives of the lower nobility, the clergy, and the cities. The purpose of the meetings was not to share power with the people but to ensure that royal decrees received the support of "the community of the realm." Edward promulgated many royal statutes that required the approval of his parliament.

Edward I's constant wars drained the treasury, but by the time of his death, the king had built up an effective bureaucracy and judicial system and a well-defined legal structure. His practice of consulting the parliaments laid the basis for democracy in England.

## The Ideal Medieval Monarch

When Louis VIII (son of Philip II Augustus) died in 1226, his widow, Blanche of Castile, became regent of France until her son Louis came of age in 1234. Louis IX was frail and pious and was regarded as a saint even in his own lifetime. He was the only king of his time to embody the ideal of the medieval monarch; he aimed to ensure peace, maintain order, and provide justice. When Pope Innocent IV tried to persuade Louis to join a crusade against Holy Roman Emperor Frederick II in 1245, the French king (clearly feeling that the pope was misguided in his intentions) refused to do battle against a fellow Christian king.

Louis IX

The French had many reasons to be content with Louis IX. The king did not participate in political misadventures that victimized the common man. On the contrary, he proved himself to be a responsible paterfamilias (father of a family), genuinely interested in law and civil justice.

He streamlined legislation, took strong action against corruption in the administration of justice, and dispatched officials to supervise the general application of his guidelines.

One of the most important reforms that Louis made was the prohibition of trial by ordeal. A remnant of Carolingian law, trial by ordeal had claimed the lives of many innocent people. Although it had been condemned by the Fourth Lateran Council in 1215, judges still ordered it as a method of resolving disputes; it was based on the belief that God would ensure victory for the righteous party. Townspeople were especially opposed to the practice; many innocent merchants had succumbed to the superior fighting skills of knights.

The French subjects believed that their monarch protected them from injustice and exploitation. This was particularly true of the communes, which Louis championed despite opposition from the aristocracy. Because of his interest in the common people, many felt that it was in their own interest to support the monarch.

The attitudes held by Louis became known beyond his realm, and his sense of justice was hailed throughout Christendom. It became common practice to put contentious matters before Louis for his consideration. He enjoyed passing judgment, and his decisions were always accepted.

Committed to the ideal of the crusades, Louis organized two expeditions, both of which failed. The first one, lasting from 1248 to 1254, landed him in Egypt (where he achieved little, due to poor strategic judgment) and then Palestine. The second one, in 1270, took him to Tunis, where the campaign was soon stranded. An epidemic broke out among the crusaders in the desert heat; Louis himself fell ill and died the same year.

Louis IX was succeeded by his son, Philip III, nicknamed Philip the Bold. During his reign (1270–1285), Philip augmented the power of the monarchy and increased the royal domains, either by annexation or by marriage. His military endeavors were less successful, however. In 1284, at the behest of Pope Martin IV, Philip crossed the Pyrenees with an army to fight Peter of Aragon but was eventually forced to retreat. He died on the way back in 1285 and was succeeded by his son, Philip IV.

## The Knights Templar

The Order of the Knights Templar was a religious order of knights set up in the early twelfth century to protect the crusaders' possessions in the Holy Land and the pilgrims who traveled to the holy places. To begin with, the knights were assigned accommodation in the palace in Jerusalem, close to the site of Solomon's Temple, from which they took their name. Skilled in all the martial arts, the knights also took a vow of chastity and poverty.

The number of Templars soon increased from the original nine, and as their fame spread, the pope took them under his direct authority. Besides protecting Christian strongholds in the Holy Land, the Templars gradually became very wealthy, as European monarchs and barons gave them lands and castles. By the middle of the thirteenth century, the order's possessions ranged from the Holy Land as far as Western Europe. Because they were able to transport gold safely throughout these regions, they began to be used as bankers, and they soon became an important and formidable financial force.

In 1291, Acre, the last city in the Holy Land to remain in the crusaders' possession, was recaptured by Muslim forces. With nothing left to protect, the Templars had lost their original purpose. Jealous of the Templars' immense wealth, many citizens in Europe were happy to circulate rumors of Templars taking part in blasphemous and heretical practices during their initiation rites. At the instigation of Philip IV of France, the Templars were persecuted, and in October of 1307, Pope Clement V ordered the arrest of every Templar in Europe. The Templars' property was either seized by the state or given to another military order, the Knights Hospitallers. Many Templars were executed; the last grand master of the order, Jacques de Molay, was burned at the stake in Paris in 1314.

A knight dressed in the garb of the Templars

## A Handsome King

Known as Philip the Fair because of his good looks and blond hair, Philip IV (ruled 1285–1314) strove to strengthen royal authority. He demanded that his nobles swear direct allegiance to him, regardless of any other feudal allegiances. His bureaucracy was run by middle-class officials who had no other loyalty than to the king himself. Appeals against legal decisions were heard in a high court of justice, known as the Parlement of Paris, in which the king's word was final. Philip also instituted assemblies, known as Estates General, which endorsed royal decisions in times of crisis. The Estates General consisted of representatives of the three "estates" (social classes)—the nobility, the clergy, and the townspeople.

Philip was aggressive in foreign policy. He waged a long war against England and even against his own fief, Flanders, which allied itself with Edward I. The conflict was ruinously expensive, and the king was staving off bankruptcy for his entire life. He devised several schemes to fill his empty treasury, including tampering with government coffers and levying new taxes.

In 1306, Philip banished all Jews from France and confiscated their money and possessions, including even the debts owed to them. As a result, many French citizens found themselves in debt to the king. The following year, Philip targeted the prosperous Knights Templar (see box, page 76). Gossip already abounded about crime and witchcraft within the order, and this was encouraged by Philip so that the royal theologians could accuse the knights of heresy. On October 13, 1307, every Templar in France was arrested. Under torture, most of the Templars confessed to the charges against them. The Order of the Knights Templar was dissolved, and most of its possessions were transferred to the king. Even money that French citizens had deposited with the order disappeared into the treasury and was never seen again by its rightful owners. Next, Philip confiscated all the possessions of the Lombard bankers, who had previously lent him money.

## The Papacy Loses Big

Church revenues had always been exempt from taxation. At the end of the thirteenth century, however, Philip decided to end this exemption.

He was not the only monarch to do so. Edward I of England was already taxing the clergy and making it clear that defaulters would be treated as outlaws.

Pope Boniface VIII (ruled 1294–1303) responded by issuing a papal bull (edict) that forbade such policies. Philip circulated a falsified version of the edict, one that presented Boniface as demanding direct political authority over the king. The French people, believing the propaganda, sided overwhelmingly with Philip. The pope subsequently issued another papal bull, demanding both spiritual and temporal power over monarchs and the right to depose the king. This played into Philip's hands.

At the French court, a lawyer named Guillaume de Nogaret presented an elaborate case against Boniface, accusing the pope of, among other things, the murder of his predecessor and keeping a devil in his house. In 1302, Philip convoked a synod of bishops that called the pope to answer those charges before a general council of prelates.

Guillaume de Nogaret was dispatched with an army to Italy to capture Boniface. Once within the Papal States, he enlisted the support of Sciarra Colonna, a local nobleman and a strong opponent of papal authority. On September 7, 1303, Guillaume and his force captured the pope in the town of Anagni. Guillaume now had to find a way to get the pope out of Italy alive, which was a problem; Colonna wanted Boniface killed on the spot. However, the townspeople of Anagni came to the aid of the pope, attacking the kidnappers and chasing them out of the country. Boniface returned to Rome and died a month later.

Pope Clement V (ruled 1305–1314) sought an end to the conflict. He came to an agreement with Philip, giving in to the king's demands. The clergy was to be taxed, in France at least. Dominium mundi no longer had any meaning. The papacy had relinquished temporal power to the secular rulers.

Nunney Castle, in Somerset, United Kingdom, was built with a focus on defense: a telling sign that in 1373, peace was difficult to find.

# CHAPTER SIX

# The Late Middle Ages: Europe in Crisis

The fourteenth century was a traumatic period for Europe, which was ravaged by a disease that killed one-third of the population. The western church split, with rival popes in Rome and Avignon, while worker unrest sowed the seeds of a new middle class.

In broad historical terms, Europe expanded during the eleventh and twelfth centuries CE. Population increased, new lands were settled, trade increased, a network of towns linked in a money economy came into being, and the boundaries of what was known as Latin Christendom became larger. Christianity spread into Scandinavia and along the Baltic coast (the Lithuanians were the last pagan people of Europe to convert; their ruler embraced Christianity in 1386).

A combination of personal ambition, military might, and religious fervor led to the political expansion of Europe. Spain was largely reconquered from the Islamic states that had ruled it from the eighth century. The Islamic presence in the central Mediterranean was destroyed, and European knights established their own states in the eastern Mediterranean around what they called the Holy Land, or Palestine. One potent symbol of this activity was the sacking of Constantinople by crusaders in 1204. At the first millennium, the year 1000 CE, the Byzantine Empire had dwarfed any European state, but at the beginning of the thirteenth century, it succumbed to the ruthless warriors of Western Europe, who were directed by the doge in Venice, the foremost trading city of the Mediterranean.

The story of Europe in the Late Middle Ages is very different. There was no such expansion; population fell, and common people rose in revolt or sought solace in new ways of seeking God. A great crisis engulfed the church.

## Christian Expansion Ends

Part of the reason for the ending of Christian expansion can be traced to external factors. In the eleventh century CE, weaknesses in the Islamic caliphates had given Christian armies an opportunity in Spain and the Middle East. By the late thirteenth century, there were strong Islamic powers that attacked the Christian presence in the Middle East. The Mamluk regime in Egypt, whose greatest leader was Sultan Baybars, destroyed the crusader states. The last crusader stronghold fell in 1302. Farther north, the Ottoman Turks created a formidable empire based in Anatolia and then expanded into southeastern Europe, defeating Serbian armies in Kosovo in 1389. Constantinople itself was spared until 1453, mainly because the Ottomans were themselves attacked by the Mongol armies of Tamerlane in the late fourteenth century.

In Eastern Europe, the boundaries of Christianity were much more stable and allowed little room for expansion. Large states—Hungary, Poland-Lithuania, and Muscovy—controlled vast stretches of land but were themselves pressed and constrained. The khanates of the Golden Horde and of the Crimea, based in the Eurasian steppes, exacted tribute and fought the Christian states.

## Death in the Guise of Famine, Disease, and War

The existence of strong external enemies was only part of the landscape of the Late Middle Ages in Europe. More important was the fall in population and the reaction to what caused that fall. Population in Europe probably peaked at between seventy and one hundred million in 1250 and remained stable for the next sixty-four years. Then, beginning in 1314, a series of bad winters resulted in poor harvests and a famine that lasted until 1322. At least one in every ten people died; it was the worst famine ever recorded in Europe. The benign climatic conditions of the previous three hundred years were changing, and the result was that agricultural yields were likely to be lower than before.

Later, in 1347, the **Black Death** arrived in Europe, spreading across the continent at an alarming speed and killing perhaps one-third of the population. The Black Death was the plague, a disease that is endemic in certain rodent populations and sometimes spreads to humans. There had been severe plagues in China in the 1330s, and trading caravans may have transferred the disease across Asia. A Genoese trading post in the Crimea was besieged by Mongol forces in 1347, and the plague was present in the town. Genoese traders fled for home, and their ships carried an epidemic that spread quickly throughout the Italian Peninsula and then into the rest of Europe.

The Black Death terrorized Europe.

The pestilence took three forms. Bubonic plague, which was usually fatal in around four days, was characterized by enlarged inflamed lymph nodes (called buboes) in the groin, armpit, or neck. Pneumonic plague, which led to an even faster death—two to three days in 90 percent of cases—infected the lungs and was transmitted between people by coughing and sneezing. When the disease spread to the blood, it became the third form, septicemic plague, which was invariably fatal, sometimes within less than twenty-four hours.

All victims of the pestilence turned a deep purple color in their last hours—hence the name, the Black Death. At the time, no one knew that the disease was spread by rodents and fleas, and as a result, people had no means of protecting themselves. The death rate became so high that it was impossible to deal with the bodies properly, and they were dumped into mass graves.

There was no cure or effective treatment for the plague in the Middle Ages, and many people thought it had been sent as a punishment from God. The clergy organized great processions of penitents; thousands took to the streets barefoot and wearing hair shirts. Many sang hymns, and some beat themselves with whips. Other people went on pilgrimages, until they were forbidden to do so by the authorities in an effort to stop the spread of the epidemic.

The plague killed around one-third of the population in Europe, and in some instances, whole villages were wiped out. At times, the crisis brought trade almost to a standstill. In the general panic, law and order broke down. Some people tried to start rebellions, while others accused the church of profiting from the inheritances left to it by the victims. The Jews were accused of having caused the epidemic by poisoning the public wells, and some of them were murdered by the terrified citizenry.

The first two years of the plague were the most devastating. Some places lost 70 percent of their inhabitants. The city of Florence, for example, had a population approaching 120,000 in 1338, but by 1351, it was reduced to only 50,000.

The Black Death reached Europe around a decade after the start of the **Hundred Years' War** between England and France. The conflict was very disruptive for the French peasantry because English forces burned villages in a deliberate scorched earth policy. As the war proceeded, bands of soldiers acted almost independently in their own interests, raiding and looting. The Hundred Years' War had repercussions in Spain and Italy as well as in France.

The effects of the catastrophic fall in population and of traumatic warfare over wide areas of Western Europe were profound. Many villages were abandoned, and there were great changes in the relationship between social classes. For example, the decline in population naturally resulted in changes in the organization of labor. Because of the increased demand for workers, many people left their villages and sought work in the towns, or simply looked for better-paid work on neighboring estates. That led to greater social and geographic mobility.

However, medieval society was not based on a free market economy. Within towns, groups of craftsmen organized in guilds became increasingly concerned with protection and exclusivity, trying to restrict the freedom of poorer workers. There were social and political clashes in many towns, especially in Italy.

In Florence, for example, the **Ciompi Rebellion** of 1378 was an uprising of workers in the woolen industry who were not part of the prosperous woolen guild. Supported by some minor guilds, they temporarily took control of the city until the guilds reunited to defeat them.

Tensions also increased in rural areas. Although, in principle, fewer workers meant higher wages or better conditions for those who were left, the authorities often tried to maintain existing wages (the Statute of Laborers in England in 1351) and to force peasants to remain on their lands. Large-scale peasant uprisings occurred in both France (the **Jacquerie** of 1358) and England (the **Peasants' Revolt** of 1381).

## The Church Under Duress

During the late fourteenth century, many people believed that the end of the world was imminent. The Black Death inspired great fear, and further horrors were widely anticipated. Some people sought to avert disaster by practicing asceticism, hoping thereby to placate God. In contrast, others indulged in every possible pleasure "while it was still possible." If ever the church was needed to console people, this was the time. Yet the church was preoccupied with a crisis of its own.

The attempts of Pope Gregory VII and his followers to reform the church in the eleventh century were only partially successful, and that success was temporary at best. The church was at the very core of medieval society, and its senior officials were part of the noble social order. It was natural that the bishops' sees (cathedral cities), abbeys, and churches fell into the hands of local rulers who possessed enough information to blackmail—and therefore to control—the electoral boards, especially because high ecclesiastical positions were usually very lucrative. Soon, taxes, inheritances, and donations were pouring into the treasury.

**Simony** (the sale of church offices to the highest bidder) became rampant, and many candidates gained sinecures (positions requiring little or no work but usually providing an income). Bishops and abbots often exploited their positions, sometimes not even bothering to take up residence at their place of office—receiving the revenues at home instead.

Clement V

The power of the papacy was further diminished during the final phase of its struggle against the emperor. Surrounded by rebellious noblemen, Pope Boniface VIII was forced to yield the right to make clerical appointments to Philip the Fair of France. Boniface's successor, Benedict XI, owed his appointment primarily to the will of the French monarch.

## Babylonian Captivity

Benedict XI died less than one year after his appointment. The cardinals then elected a Frenchman, who chose the name Clement V. However, Clement would never set foot in either Rome or the Vatican.

In Italy, a chaotic battle was raging between two factions, the Guelphs and the Ghibellines. Clement V, who had little desire to become involved in this hornets' nest, stayed in France. In 1309, he ended up in the city of Avignon, which, together with the surrounding territory, had been given to the Holy See. Avignon was part of the Holy Roman Empire, but only the Rhone River separated it from the kingdom of France. Clement was thus close enough to French territory to be able to rely on the protection of the king of France.

The popes remained in Avignon for more than sixty years. During this period, the papal throne was always occupied by a Frenchman. Some historians claim that the Avignon papacy was merely a French puppet administration, but there is conflicting evidence with regard to its political independence. The period was named the **Babylonian Captivity** by the Italian poet Petrarch (1304–1374), who campaigned to have the popes return to the Vatican.

During the Babylonian Captivity, the entire papal administration operated out of the huge Papal Palace at Avignon. Over the years, it grew into a vast bureaucracy; Avignon became a gigantic administrative office in which everyone knew his place and his duties. The working methods were cumbersome and slow, and corruption managed to work its way up to the highest levels of the system. Anyone who looked to this administration for justice usually looked in vain. The popes were politicians rather than spiritual leaders, and their principal occupation was seeing to the maintenance of an effective bureaucracy.

The popes constantly sought new sources of income. They took possession of claims and inheritances, they were easily bribed, and they practiced simony on a large scale. As a result, the papacy lost much of its prestige. Calls for reform became increasingly urgent, and during the Hundred Years' War, a company of soldiers invaded the Papal Palace and refused to leave until a ransom was paid to them.

## Return to Rome

In the absence of the popes, Rome lost most of the pilgrims who had historically been its main source of revenue. The city and the surrounding countryside became almost ungovernable, but energetic cardinals sent from Avignon brought order to the area, and by the middle of the fourteenth century, much of the anarchy had been reduced. A few years later, papal authority in Italy had been sufficiently restored for the pope to play a significant role in Italian politics, which greatly disturbed Rome's neighbors in the north. Under the leadership of the powerful city of Florence, an antipope league was formed. However, it encountered unexpected resistance when another Italian movement arose demanding the pope's return to Rome.

Ordinary Italian citizens and the clergy bombarded the pope, Gregory XI (ruled 1370–1378), with petitions requesting that he return to Rome. These petitions persuaded the pope to move back to Rome in early 1377, but his stay was such a disaster that he soon fled back to Avignon. He returned to Rome in late 1377 and remained there until his death. Although the move marked the return of the popes to Rome, the papal administration and most of the cardinals

Pope Urban VI, seen here on the right, worsened the divide within the Catholic Church.

remained in Avignon.

Following the death of Gregory XI in 1378, a new pope was elected in response to demands from the Roman people for an Italian pope. The fearful cardinals hastily chose the archbishop of Bari, who became Pope Urban VI. The cardinals in Avignon pledged their allegiance, and once more, an Italian pope resided in the Holy City.

## The Western Schism

Urban was no diplomat, and he rapidly alienated several of his own supporters. In 1389, the newly hostile cardinals withdrew to Anagni, where they announced that Urban's election had been unduly influenced by popular intimidation and was therefore invalid.

A new election was held, and the dissidents elected another pope, Clement VII, who took up residence at Avignon. Urban refused to accept Clement's election and remained in Rome, condemning the rebellious cardinals. The western church was in **schism**.

Christendom was in turmoil. The competing popes issued contradictory decrees and hurled bulls of excommunication at each other. The worldly rulers profited from the schism by recognizing the pope who supported their interests. Naples, France, Aragon, Castile, Portugal, Savoy, Scotland, and several German kingdoms took the side of Clement VII in Avignon. Urban VI in Rome won the support of northern Italy, England, Hungary, and the Scandinavian kingdoms. Professors at the University of Paris advocated neutrality, and their advice was followed by some kings and religious orders.

The church schism of the fourteenth century caused chaos, but it also had some positive effects. The existence of two popes made it clear that drastic reforms were needed in the church. As intellectuals began to debate the need for reform, popular preachers became involved. Some clerics, such as **Jan Hus** in Bohemia (see box, page 90), were accused of heresy when they preached social revolution. However, reforms were instituted in several places.

The western schism lasted for thirty-nine years, during which time two powerful popes ruled in Avignon and five ruled in Rome. Urban VI again displayed his talent for making enemies when he excommunicated the king of Naples, who could have been a powerful ally. A similar fate awaited Carl of Durazzo, who led a crusade within Italy to increase Urban's power. By the end of Urban's reign, he had been abandoned by all of his cardinals, and he died, unlamented, in 1389.

The popes in Avignon fared no better. After the death of Clement VII in 1394, the fanatical Pedro de Luna came to power as Benedict XIII. He was an arrogant man and a fierce ruler who spared no one, least of all the king of France, who responded in 1398 by besieging Avignon and forcing the pope to flee, first to Perpignan and later to a castle in his native Aragon.

Christians everywhere sought a solution to the problems in the church. The University of Paris suggested that one of the popes should resign. Attempts were made to open negotiations, but the two pontiffs refused to meet each other. Another proposal was that the two popes should appoint an independent tribunal, but, again, they refused to cooperate.

## The Council Theory

A majority of the cardinals decided to hold a council in Pisa, and this assembly of prelates, meeting in 1409, came to the conclusion that the popes in Rome and Avignon were displaying signs of heretical stubbornness. The assembly declared both popes deposed and elected a new pope. However, because neither of the other popes had the slightest intention of stepping down, the church now had three popes.

The council of cardinals set a dangerous precedent. For the first time, prelates had solved a problem on their own, without consulting the pope. That gave rise to the council theory, which maintained that a council was a higher ecclesiastical authority than the Holy Father.

## Reformer Jan Hus

Jan Hus was a leading advocate of church reform during the early fifteenth century, when Christendom was in disarray over the western schism. Hus was born in southern Bohemia (present-day Czech Republic) in 1372 and graduated from Prague University in 1394. At that time, around half the land in Bohemia was owned by the church, and many of the higher clergy held multiple offices, making them extremely wealthy. Discontent among the lower clergy and the peasantry fostered widespread calls for reform in the church, and Hus, who had begun to teach at the university, became a leading advocate for a radical shake-up of church practices.

In 1402, Hus took charge of the Bethlehem Chapel, which was the hotbed of a national reform movement founded by Jan Milic. Here, sermons were preached in Czech, instead of Latin, and Hus's sermons became increasingly radical in tone. He constantly attacked clerical corruption, and in 1409, he was excommunicated by the archbishop of Prague. Undeterred, Hus continued his preaching, targeting especially the widespread practice of the sale of indulgences, which had become a scandal. An indulgence was a document that promised the purchaser he would escape suffering for his sins in purgatory, and the sale of these documents raised a great deal of money for the church.

In 1412, Hus was excommunicated again. For the next two years, he took refuge in the castles of friends in southern Bohemia, where he busied himself writing treatises on church matters. When the **Council of Constance** was convened, Hus was invited by the Holy Roman emperor to attend and put forward his views. Hus was reluctant to put himself in danger, but the emperor promised him a safe conduct (there and back), so Hus agreed to go. Despite the promise of a safe conduct, Hus was arrested soon after his arrival in Constance and was subsequently tried for heresy. He was condemned to death and burned at the stake.

Woodcut of Jan Hus from the *Schedelsche Weltchronik*, or *Schedel's World Chronicle*, published in 1493

The council theory was fiercely opposed by all three popes, even John XXII, the pope elected by the council of Pisa. As the council theory gained in popularity, John looked to the German emperor, Louis of Bavaria, for support. The emperor, however, thought that none of the three popes was worthy of the office, and he wanted to convene a new council. A majority of the cardinals favored that idea, and under his auspices, another council was held in Constance (modern Konstanz, Germany).

Convened in 1415, the Council of Constance was open to bishops, cardinals, university professors, and royal representatives, all of whom were given the right to vote. The council issued a decree of *Sacrosancta*, which explicitly affirmed that the decrees of a church council would override those of the pope. John XXII realized that he had no choice but to resign. Gregory XII also gave up his position voluntarily, but it was impossible to convince Benedict XIII to do the same. Therefore, the council dismissed Benedict, and he, along with four loyal cardinals, retreated to a castle in his native Aragon, where he spent the rest of his life issuing bulls of excommunication against anyone who did not recognize him as pope.

For the next two years, the Council of Constance remained the top ecclesiastical authority in western Christendom. In 1417, the council elected Cardinal Odo Colonna, who then became Pope Martin V. Martin took up residence in Rome and immediately distanced himself from the tenets of the council theory. Although he accepted certain reforms made by the council, he categorically rejected the idea that he had to submit to the decisions of the prelates. The Council of Constance also issued a decree that it should convene regularly, but Martin disapproved of that idea, too.

In 1431, just a few weeks before Martin died, a new council was convened in the city of Basel. Martin's successor, Eugenius IV (ruled 1431–1447), tried to adjourn the council, but its members refused, reiterating the decree of *Sacrosancta*—that the powers of the council superseded those of the pope. After years of bickering, the pope transferred the council to Ferrara in 1437, but some members remained in Basel, acting as a rebel council. The prelates in Basel decided to dismiss Eugenius and elect yet another pope, a move that gave Eugenius an excellent argument against the council theory. The pope claimed that the churchmen in Basel had caused another schism, and he insisted on the concept of his own supreme authority. Most of Christendom accepted this, and the council theory sank into oblivion.

Church unity was restored, but the situation was otherwise virtually unchanged. Reforms were not implemented because it was not in the best interest of the popes to do so. During the remainder of the fifteenth century, the popes helped their followers to obtain lucrative positions, appointed family members to high office, and generally led lives of luxury while continuing their political involvements.

## Art Thrives

While much of the Late Middle Ages in Europe was characterized by political decline and degeneration, there was a great flowering of civilization. In Italy, for example, the rediscovery of classical models and the patronage of city-states led to the great artistic achievements of what later ages called the Renaissance. In fifteenth-century CE Burgundy, the dukes were great patrons of the arts. In Portugal, attempts to explore the Atlantic Ocean and the coast of Africa under the energetic sponsorship of Henry the Navigator opened up enormous new vistas for European enterprise. Many towns and cities in northern Europe prospered. Nevertheless, the medieval world (with its settled social order, based on feudalism, underpinned by common religious values, and defended by a class of mounted warriors) was undeniably crumbling.

Leagues and alliances became essential to survival during the fifteenth century. Here, the Krögelstein Castle is destroyed by the Swabian League.

# CHAPTER SEVEN

# Anarchy, Conflict, Leagues, and Alliances

During the fifteenth century, Europe evolved politically and culturally into something like its modern form. However, the continent emerged from the Middle Ages slowly and painfully, and the speed of progress varied greatly from region to region.

By the end of the fifteenth century, the borders of the early modern period had been drawn. Spain, France, and England had become centralized monarchies. The kingdom of Burgundy, incorporating much of the Low Countries (modern Belgium and Netherlands), was a center of culture. The cities of northern Italy fostered learning and the arts, giving rise to the Renaissance, while continued dissent within the church led to the Reformation and religious wars in the north.

However, the end of the Middle Ages was an era of strife throughout Europe: Italy fell into anarchy; armed conflicts raged in Spain; and famine, starvation, and plague were widespread. In spite of the chaos and misery, royal power in Spain, France, and England was not eroded because the authority of the king in each country was no longer in question. Before the formation of centralized monarchic governments, feudal vassals had constantly sought to win power from the sovereign. Over the course of the Middle Ages, the nobles increasingly supported their rulers.

## After the Holy Roman Empire

In the twelfth and thirteenth centuries, it had seemed possible that the Holy Roman Empire would come to dominate the whole of Europe. However, imperial power faded until the German Empire divided into a patchwork of states. In the center of the old empire, there were several small counties; in the south, larger territorial kingdoms were established in Austria, Bavaria, Bohemia, Saxony, and Swabia. An interesting development was the Swiss Confederation, which consisted of several communities of farmers who had settled in various valleys in the Alps. Each part of the confederation had its own government, constitution, courts, and coinage. The confederation was based simply on an oath of mutual aid and assistance against aggressors. The arrangement was formalized in 1481.

Another alliance was the Swabian League of Cities, which was formed in 1331, when twenty-two cities united under the protection of Louis of Bavaria. The league had mixed fortunes over the next century and a half, as nobles strove to curb the cities' power. In 1488, the **Great Swabian League**, formed under the protection of the emperor Frederick III, incorporated cities of Swabia, the Rhineland, Bavaria, and Franconia. Another important alliance was the Hanseatic League (see box, page 99), which was formed to promote trade interests.

## The Political Geography of Italy

Under Frederick II (ruled 1215–1250), Italy had become polarized. The south consisted of the kingdoms of Naples and Sicily, which had centralized governments controlled by the emperor. In the north, Frederick and his successors lost control of Lombardy and the Papal States, and the cities of both regions became independent.

The main Italian city-states that emerged were Florence, Mantua, Milan, and Venice. City expansion also occurred in the Papal States, where Bologna, Ferrara, and Perugia became independent and powerful.

The Italian cities were constantly at war over their boundaries, and because the citizenry consisted mainly of merchants and bankers, their armies consisted of mercenaries called condottieri.

Milan and Florence were ruled over, respectively, by the Visconti family and the Medici family. Most of the Viscontis were tyrants, but in the middle of the fifteenth century, they were succeeded by Francesco Sforza, a benevolent ruler and a noted patron of the arts. Under Sforza and his successors, Milan became home to some of the greatest artists and sculptors of the Italian Renaissance, including Leonardo da Vinci.

Milan, however, was eclipsed by Florence under the Medicis, wealthy bankers who fostered the leading artists and architects of the age. The most famous member of the family was Lorenzo de' Medici (Lorenzo the Magnificent), who ruled Florence in the second half of the fifteenth century. He nurtured many leading artists, including the young Michelangelo.

## Northern Europe and Scandinavia

In the early Middle Ages, Scandinavia was sparsely populated, but by the eleventh century CE, the major population centers were established and the present-day states of Norway, Denmark, and Sweden were beginning to emerge.

The Norwegians were aggressive seafarers who, during the Viking era, had explored the North Atlantic Ocean and raided and settled in Scotland, Ireland, the Orkney and Shetland Islands, and the Hebrides. During succeeding centuries, they launched military expeditions to safeguard their possessions. In 1260, the Norwegian Empire reached its greatest extent when it incorporated Iceland.

In 1266, King Magnus VI of Norway ceded the Hebrides and the Isle of Man to Scotland in return for the Scots' recognition of the Norwegian claim to the Orkney and Shetland islands. In 1294, a blockade by the Hanseatic League forced Magnus's son, Eric II (ruled 1280–1299), to allow the league to monopolize trade south of Bergen, while the Norwegians retained control of Iceland and Greenland.

The Hanseatic League was becoming unpopular in Sweden as well. German merchants from Lübeck, the largest Hanseatic port on the Baltic coast, were exempted from Swedish customs duties in the twelfth century, and by 1225, they had established the Community of German Visitors at Visby in Sweden. In an effort to restrict further growth of Hanseatic power, the Scandinavian kings allied against the league, and a series of battles ensued. Hostilities were eventually

Queen Margaret

ended in 1370 by the Treaty of Stralsund, which restored revenues and castles to the members of the league.

Meanwhile, the three Scandinavian countries were moving slowly toward unification. In 1322, Magnus Erickson was crowned king of both Norway and Sweden, but the two countries split soon afterward. A more lasting effect was produced by Waldemar IV, who came to the throne of Denmark in 1340. His daughter, Margaret, who was heir to the Danish crown and wife of King Haakon VI of Norway and Sweden, made the unification a fact.

Waldemar died in 1375. Margaret then became regent of Denmark on behalf of her son, Olaf IV, in 1376. She was appointed to the same position in Norway in 1380. The Swedish king, Albert of Mecklenburg, faced fierce opposition from a group of disaffected nobles, and in 1389, Margaret joined forces with the rebels to defeat Albert at the Battle of Lonkoping. After that victory, Sweden recognized Margaret as queen.

Olaf IV had died in 1387, leaving Margaret as regent without a successor. To resolve that problem, she named her fifteen-year-old great-nephew, Eric of Pomerania, as Olaf's heir in 1389. In 1397, it was agreed that the three Scandinavian kingdoms should unite under a single sovereign. Each country was to maintain its own institutions, while subscribing to a common foreign policy. The royal succession was to be agreed by common consent. Eric was then crowned king of Scandinavia at Kalmar, although in practice, Margaret continued to rule until her death in 1412.

## The Hanseatic League

The Hanseatic League of north German cities was a union of free cities that promoted their own interests in trade, with representatives in London, the Scandinavian countries, and Poland.

A fourteenth century Hanseatic League ship

It had its origins in the twelfth century, when groups of merchants (called *hansas*) banded together to travel through dangerous territory to annual markets. In due course, the hansa concept came to denote a group of cities rather than just a group of merchants. By the middle of the thirteenth century, the Hanseatic League emerged as a powerful federation that played a role in political affairs as well as in trade. The number of members continued to grow until the fifteenth century, when more than a hundred cities were members. The leading Hanseatic centers included Bremen, Gdansk, Hamburg, Lübeck, Riga, Stockholm, and Szczecin.

The advantages of membership were numerous. The league had trading posts in London, Bergen, Bruges, and the Russian city of Novgorod. German merchants migrated to Scandinavia, Poland, and the Baltic coast of Russia, setting up powerful merchant colonies that gradually eliminated competition. However, the league had an important enemy: the king of Denmark. The Danish king controlled the Sont Strait (the passage between the Baltic Sea and the North Sea) and demanded tolls from passing ships.

The league refused to pay, and as a result, there were several wars until the league finally won exemption in 1370.

The Union of Kalmar did not endure. Sweden broke away in the fifteenth century, but Denmark and Norway continued to be a political unit until the early nineteenth century.

## Poland Searches for Allies

The Polish kingdom emerged in the eleventh century. During the twelfth century, German merchants from the Hanseatic League established settlements in the region. In spite of resistance from native Slavs, the Germans took over Pomerania and Silesia, and by the thirteenth century, Poland was divided and overrun by Germans. Many free peasants from Germany and the Netherlands immigrated to Poland and set up new towns that resisted all efforts at integration with the Polish state.

In the early fourteenth century, King Wladyslaw I (ruled 1306–1333) achieved some success in subduing his German citizens, but he was forced to accept the loss of much of his land to German merchants, the king of Bohemia, and the Teutonic Knights.

Wladyslaw II

To help withstand the German threat, Poland sought an alliance with the kingdom of Hungary, but their pact ended in disaster; the two countries did not have sufficient interests in common. The only alternative left to the Poles was to join forces with pagan Lithuania, which was constantly under threat from the Teutonic Knights.

In 1385, Jadwiga, the twelve-year-old queen of Poland, married the Lithuanian grand duke Jagiello, who converted to Christianity and took the name Wladyslaw II. The marriage united the two countries against their common foe. At the Battle of Tannenberg in 1410, the combined forces of Poland and Lithuania defeated the

Florence flourished in the birth of the Renaissance.

## The Renaissance Begins

The fourteenth and fifteenth centuries saw the birth of new ideas in society, government, and artistic development. Society was based increasingly on urban industry and international trade instead of agriculture, and more power fell into the hands of the bourgeois class.

The royal, ducal, and papal courts became centers of culture. New ideas sprang from the late medieval experiences of communal governments and from the loss of confidence in royalty and the papacy resulting from the Hundred Years' War, the papal schism, and the crusades. There was also renewed interest in Italy's rich heritage and in classical learning and culture, spurred by the reintroduction of texts (through Arabic Spain) to European universities in the thirteenth century.

The Renaissance first took hold in the cities of northern Italy. In northern Europe, scholars became engaged in questioning the tenets of the Catholic Church, a development that eventually led to the Reformation.

## The Order of the Teutonic Knights

Founded in 1198 CE, the Order of the Teutonic Knights emerged from the German branch of the Knights Hospitallers. The Teutonic Knights had first set out to Christianize Palestine, but as crusading declined in the thirteenth century, the order turned its attention to the pagans in the Baltic regions. The order was first invited into Poland in 1226 to help settle internal conflicts and unite the kingdom. Once there, the knights established their headquarters at Marienburg (near Gdansk) and set about organizing the conquest of the Slavic territories. Many enthusiastic European noblemen joined the order, keen to advance the causes of Christianity and Germany against the Slavs. The result of these campaigns was the formation of the Baltic Empire, which extended as far north as Lithuania, Latvia, Estonia, and Russia and survived until the sixteenth century.

Teutonic Knights defend Baumburg in 1231.

Teutonic Knights, thereby ending two centuries of domination by the order in the region.

## Mongolian Warriors

In the early thirteenth century, Mongol horsemen from central Asia swept westward over the northern European plain. They overran the great Russian kingdoms in a single massive assault and reached the first settlements of German colonists in 1240. Novgorod was a powerful merchant city, but its prince, Alexander Nevsky (ruled 1236–1263), did not dare to confront the powerful **Mongols**. Instead, he made peace with them and agreed to pay an annual tribute.

The Mongols then destroyed the city of Kiev and advanced westward until they confronted a combined force of Poles and Teutonic Knights at the Battle of Liegnitz in 1241. Although the Mongols triumphed, they suffered heavy losses and subsequently withdrew to the vast Russian plain.

In the late fifteenth century, Ivan the Great (Ivan III) repelled the Mongols, annexed Russian principalities, and founded Muscovy, a new Russian state.

The Battle of Sluys marked the beginning of the Hundred Years' War.

CHAPTER EIGHT

# A Century of War

The Hundred Years' War actually lasted for 116 years. When the war began, in 1337, the English had a powerful presence in France and sought to extend their influence. By the war's end, in 1453, the only English holding in France was **Calais**.

The Hundred Years' War between France and England in the fourteenth and fifteenth centuries had many causes. The kings of England had claims to French lands, particularly Gascony in the southwest. The English also competed with the French for control of Flanders. There was, in addition, the question of who should sit on the French throne.

In 1328, the French king, Charles IV, died and left no sons to inherit his realm. Edward III of England (the son of Charles's sister) promptly claimed the French throne. The French nobility, horrified at the prospect of being ruled by an English king, hastily rediscovered an ancient law that forbade inheritance through a woman. They chose Philip of Valois, the late king's cousin, to succeed him as Philip VI. For a time, Edward appeared to accept that situation.

England's economic ties with France and Flanders were strong. The region around Bordeaux guaranteed a steady supply of cheap wine, for which the English had a particular liking, and the textile weavers of Flanders depended on imports of English wool. The count of Flanders was a vassal of the French king, and in the event of a conflict between France and England, the count might prohibit the import of English wool, seriously damaging the English economy. On the other hand, the English king might impoverish Flanders by banning wool exports. However, the rich and powerful burghers of Flanders were aware of the economic realities and were sympathetic to the aspirations of the English court. Consequently, when the burghers rebelled against the Francophile count, they did so with the encouragement of the English king.

## Burgeoning Hostilities

Hostilities began in 1337, when Philip VI confiscated Edward III's fief of Gascony. In retaliation, Edward immediately proclaimed himself king of France and assembled an army.

In Flanders, the count ordered the arrest of all resident Englishmen. Edward responded by halting wool exports, and that move caused massive unemployment in the Flemish towns. In Ghent, the workers rebelled, and the uprising caught on in other cities, which forced the count to flee to France in 1339.

In the absence of the count, control of Flanders passed to rebel leader Jacob van Artevelde, a Ghent aristocrat and merchant. Van Artevelde's vision for Flanders was a close federation of city-states under the protection of an English king who was officially recognized as the ruler of France. Edward III and his army landed on the Flemish coast in February of 1340, and in June, an English squadron swept the French fleet from the estuary of Sluys, near Bruges, thus ensuring the safety of imports of wool.

Van Artevelde never realized his dream. French agents promoted dissension among the Flemish, and the urban aristocracy turned against the guildsmen who constituted the backbone of the rebellion. The count returned to Flanders, winning the support of the rural nobility, and Jacob van Artevelde, who was proving to be a tyrant, encountered increasing difficulty in maintaining his position. During a weavers' rebellion in Ghent in 1345, van Artevelde was murdered by the crowd, leaving the way clear for the count to resume full control of Flanders.

## The Battle of Crécy

Having lost influence in Flanders and being unable to enter Gascony (which was under French occupation), Edward III invaded France. In July of 1346, he landed on the Normandy coast and plundered Caen.

## KEY SITES IN THE HUNDRED YEARS' WAR

He then marched on Paris, but failing to capture the capital, he was forced to head back north. He took up a position for battle near **Crécy** on the road to Dunkirk.

The ensuing battle was a catastrophic defeat for the French (see box, page 108). It was the first time that French cavalry had been confronted by English longbowmen, and the deadly rain of arrows

## Military Strategy at the Battle of Crécy

Edward III's army consisted of around twenty thousand men, of whom ten thousand were archers—all armed with English longbows, which had great advantages over the crossbows used by the French. A longbow was around 6 feet (1.8 meters) long and had a range of around 250 yards (230 m), which was around twice that of a crossbow. The longbow could also be fired much more rapidly than the crossbow; a proficient archer could shoot between six and twelve arrows per minute.

Edward's strategy was to separate his troops into three divisions, each consisting of dismounted knights, foot soldiers, and archers. One division was placed in the center, with the other two divisions on the wings. Rows of sharpened wooden stakes were driven into the ground in front of the divisions to protect them from cavalry charges.

On the evening of August 26, 1346, Philip of France, with an army of sixty thousand men, arrived on the field. Philip sent his crossbowmen in first, but they encountered such a devastating hail of arrows from the English archers that they retreated. The French cavalry that was following trampled many of them to death.

As the French cavalrymen reached the English lines, they were stopped short by the sharpened stakes. The English men-at-arms surged out from behind the stakes and slew many of the French knights before they had time to turn. Meanwhile, successive French cavalry charges came under deadly fire from the longbow men on either flank. By the end of the day, thousands of Frenchmen lay dead on the field, including 1,500 knights and nobles. Philip's brother, Charles II of Alençon, was among the dead, as were King John of Bohemia and Louis II de Nevers (count of Flanders), both allies of the French king. There are no reliable figures for English losses, but they are generally agreed to have been comparatively light, perhaps no more than 250 dead.

destroyed wave after wave of mounted charges. Philip was wounded but managed to escape from the field; Edward took his victorious army north to besiege Calais.

After a year's siege, Edward captured Calais, which became an important English foothold in France. For the next ten years, the Black Death ravaged all of Europe. France and England suspended their hostilities while the plague was at its height.

## John II, Marcel, and the Dauphin

When fighting resumed in 1355, Edward III's son, Edward (the Black Prince), led raids in southwestern France, plundering, burning, and destroying crops over vast areas. The following year, the Black Prince campaigned in central France, where he defeated a French army at the Battle of **Poitiers** on September 19. The English took many prisoners, including the French king John II, who had succeeded Philip VI in 1350. John was taken to England and imprisoned in the Tower of London.

The capture of John II (called the Good) heralded the start of four years of riots in France. Revolution had been in the air since 1355, when John had summoned the Estates General to authorize yet more taxes to finance the continuing war against the English. The Paris provost of merchants, Étienne Marcel, had proposed that the assembly should be responsible for administering the money. After John's capture, Marcel headed a hostile meeting of the Estates General that proposed dismissing corrupt officials and placing the crown prince (the oldest son of the King of France, known as the dauphin) under its authority. The dauphin reluctantly signed a document authorizing a major program of administrative reform.

After the meeting of the Estates General was disbanded, Marcel took control of the government of Paris. He ruled efficiently, organizing the citizens into military companies.

Meanwhile, revolutionary fervor spread to the countryside. To the north and northeast of Paris, bands of peasants stormed through the rural areas, raiding their lords' castles and killing everyone they considered to be an opponent. Although the uprising caused widespread alarm among the landowners, it had little chance of success. The peasants had no real plan and were poorly organized. Within a few weeks, the rebellion was over.

It was Charles II (called Charles the Bad), king of Navarre, who ultimately restored order. He presented himself as regent (because the dauphin was only eighteen years old), and most of the landowners gratefully accepted his help, although his involvement was viewed with deep suspicion by Marcel.

Having left Paris after the assassination of his marshals, the dauphin set about enlisting the support of honest monarchists who could not tolerate restrictions on royal power and who identified the crown with opposition to the English. When the dauphin advanced to Compiègne and summoned a session of the Estates of Champagne, seeking money, they gave it to him. Marcel began to lose his following, and in 1358, he was killed by a monarchist.

## Peace Negotiations and the Treaty of Bretigny

The dauphin then returned to Paris and turned his attention to foreign policy. Edward III, still determined to claim the French crown, had penetrated into Burgundy. Realizing that his weakened kingdom had little chance of defeating the English in battle, the dauphin opened peace negotiations in 1360, which resulted in the Treaty of Bretigny. In exchange for relinquishing his claims on the French throne, Edward was to receive Aquitaine (almost one-third of the area of France), which he would hold outright and not as a vassal of the French king. The French also agreed to pay a large ransom for the return of John II, although he died before he could be released.

The dauphin, now Charles V of France, was a clear thinker with admirable perseverance who had shown his ability to resolve a crisis. He surrounded himself with able counselors, who treated government almost as if it were a science.

Charles V worked hard to rebuild his country and earned himself the honorific Charles the Wise. After the Peace of Bretigny, the many mercenaries who had fought for both sides were no longer needed; having been discharged, they roamed the roads as highway robbers. Charles appointed Bertrand du Guesclin of Gascony to command his army, and when Charles took sides in the civil war raging in Castile (part of modern Spain), Bertrand rounded up the highwaymen and led them across the Pyrenees. They again encountered their old enemy, the Black Prince, who was fighting to restore Peter the Cruel to the throne of Castile.

The peace in France was disrupted when the barons in Gascony rebelled against their English overlords. When Charles took up their cause, Edward III invaded France once more in 1367. However, the French strategy had changed. Instead of seeking to confront the English in battle, Bertrand du Guesclin employed guerrilla tactics, using his highwaymen to harass the English forces with frequent raids and ambushes. During the next ten years, the French wore the English down with this policy, and by the time Edward died in 1377, his possessions in France had been reduced to Bordeaux, Bayonne, and Calais—little more than the territories he had held at the beginning of the war, forty years earlier.

In 1380, a new crisis forced both countries to suspend hostilities. Charles the Wise died, and both England and France entered a period of rebellion and civil war.

## Rebellion and Unrest

In France, Charles V was succeeded by his twelve-year-old son, Charles VI. In England, the new king, Richard II (grandson of Edward III), was a teenager. Both countries were ruled by regents.

In England, there was great social upheaval. The peasants, craftsmen, and some of the lower clergy were resentful of the punitive taxes levied to finance the war with France, and they were ready to fight for their cause in 1381. Under the bold leadership of Wat Tyler, a group of rebels made their way to London, where they confronted Richard II. However, the rebellion was quickly put down.

In France, bands of robbers continued to ravage the countryside, and the population had to deal with repeated plague epidemics. Charles VI went mad, and in 1393, he was replaced by his younger brother, Louis, who became regent.

In England, Richard II faced opposition from powerful barons, who incited the parliament to pass measures that limited the king's authority. Richard retaliated by confiscating the estates of his leading opponents, who included Henry Bolingbroke, his cousin. In 1399, while Richard was absent in Ireland, Bolingbroke raised an army and

## Wat Tyler

Wat Tyler was the leader of the Peasants' Revolt, a widespread English uprising in 1381. The causes of discontent can be traced back to the onset of the Black Death, which killed almost one-third of the population in the mid-fourteenth century. Workers were in short supply, and consequently, wages rose. To counteract this, the parliament passed a statue in 1351 to restrict wage increases. The peasants, naturally, opposed the law, and their resentments boiled over in 1380, when yet another tax was imposed to pay for the wars with France.

Rebellion first flared in Essex and soon reached Kent, where the rebels chose Wat Tyler as their leader. At the head of a band of peasants, Tyler marched on Canterbury and captured it on June 10, 1381. The rebels then turned toward London, growing in numbers to between sixty thousand and one hundred thousand. When they reached the capital, they plundered and burned many buildings, including the house of John of Gaunt (the king's uncle) and the Newgate and Fleet prisons, where they released the prisoners.

Much alarmed, the fourteen-year-old king, Richard II, arranged to meet the rebels at Mile End, to the east of the city. He agreed to redress their grievances, which included the requirement of feudal service and the imposition of exorbitant taxes. However, in spite of the king's concessions, the rebels went on to capture the Tower of London and to kill the archbishop of Canterbury.

When the king met the rebels again the following day, June 15, at Smithfield in London, Tyler made further demands, including that there should be no more serfdom and that all church property should be confiscated and distributed among the members of each parish. According to a chronicle of the time, Tyler behaved with overfamiliarity to the king, taking his hand and saying: "Brother, be of good comfort and joyful, for you shall have praise from the commons even more than you have yet had, and we shall be good companions."

During the meeting, a scuffle broke out and the lord mayor of London inflicted some grievous wounds on Tyler. The rebel leader was taken by his followers to nearby St. Bartholomew's Hospital, but the mayor later found him there and had him dragged out into the middle of Smithfield, where he was beheaded. After Tyler's death, the rebellion quickly collapsed. Richard reneged on all his promises, and many of the rebels were hanged.

John Ball, a revolutionary priest, is shown on horseback encouraging the peasants with Wat Tyler, shown here in red.

seized the crown, forcing Richard to abdicate. Bolingbroke then ruled England as Henry IV.

Meanwhile, French barons competed to fill the power vacuum that was created by the king's insanity. When John the Fearless, Duke of Burgundy, had Louis killed in 1407, civil war broke out. The Burgundians allied with the English, setting the scene for the final phase of the Hundred Years' War.

## Henry V and Charles VII

Henry V came to the throne of England in 1413. He took the opportunity afforded by the civil war in France to renew his claim to the French crown. In 1415, he landed on the Normandy coast, took the city of Harfleur, and then defeated French forces at the Battle of Agincourt.

Henry V's victory increased the power of his ally, John the Fearless, Duke of Burgundy. Meanwhile, as Henry continued his campaign in Normandy, the rival French factions began to consider a truce. In 1419, the duke of Burgundy arranged to meet with the dauphin (son of the mad king) to discuss terms. They met on the bridge at Montereau, just outside Paris, but supporters on both sides began to hurl insults; swords were drawn, and the duke was slain.

The murderer had not served his side well. Philip the Good, who succeeded his father as duke of Burgundy, was equally pro-English. Anxious to put an end to the conflicts in France, he negotiated the Treaty of Troyes with Henry V. Under this treaty, which was signed in 1419 CE, France was partitioned between England, Burgundy, and the dauphin (who was then disinherited in favor of Henry V).

For a while, the future looked hopeless for Charles, the disinherited dauphin, but his prospects improved dramatically when both his father, Charles VI, and Henry V of England died in the same year, 1422.

The new king of England, Henry VI, was only nine months old, so the duke of Bedford acted as regent. In the king's name, the duke controlled the French regions from his domain in Paris. Charles VII, the new French king (in name only), held court in the town of Bourges. His enemies called him the king of Bourges, and the idea that he would one day rule the whole of France seemed remote. Pessimism

Joan of Arc led the forces of France to victory and is shown here arriving at the Chateau de Chinon.

spread throughout France, where the people had experienced nothing for decades but misery, oppression, and poverty. However, there was a flicker of hope.

## Joan of Arc

In October of 1428, following a victory at Verneuil, the English laid siege to Orléans. If they could take the city, it would be a vital link between their territories to the north and south of the Loire River. The French held out for months, but in the spring of 1429, the city seemed close to surrender. It was at that point that Joan of Arc (the Maid of Orléans) finally made her miraculous intervention.

**Joan of Arc** was a peasant girl, born in 1412 in Domrémy in Lorraine, which at that time was not considered part of France. At age thirteen, Joan started to have visions and to hear what she called her voices (the voices of Saint Michael, Saint Catherine, and Saint Margaret) directing her to go to France in the name of God. The voices,

## St. Crispin's Day: Battle of Agincourt

After capturing Harfleur, Henry V planned to take his army back to England to escape the epidemic of dysentery that had broken out in the city. On October 8, 1415, his troops left Harfleur, heading for Calais and carrying rations for eight days. At the Somme River, they were delayed by floods and were not able to cross until October 18. By October 24, when they met the French on the road to Calais, the English had marched 260 miles (416 kilometers) in seventeen days; they were exhausted and hungry, and many of them had succumbed to dysentery.

At dawn on October 25 (St. Crispin's Day), the two armies took up their positions on opposite sides of a newly plowed field. Because it had been raining continuously for two weeks, the field eventually became a sea of mud, in which many fallen men drowned. As had been the battle plan at Crécy, Henry divided his forces into three parts, with archers on the two flanks. For protection, huge stakes were driven into the ground and pointed at the enemy.

Having taken up their positions, the two armies waited for more than four hours. Eventually, Henry ordered his forces to advance to within longbow range, where they unleashed volley after volley of arrows. The French cavalrymen charged, but many of them fell in the mud before they reached the English lines; those who got through were cut down or taken prisoner. A subsequent charge by French foot soldiers fared no better; their advance was obstructed by fallen horses and knights. A second French infantry charge was seriously hampered by the piles of bodies in front of the English positions, and many more Frenchmen were killed or taken prisoner.

As the French commanders tried to rally their troops for a third attack, Henry ordered that the prisoners should be killed. That command was given partly because the number of prisoners taken was so great that a large portion of the English army was tied up in guarding them. Henry may also have feared that the prisoners would turn on their captors. Whatever the reason, the move was extremely

The Battle of Argincourt, depicted above, is forever immortalized in Shakespeare's Henry V, with Henry rallying his outnumbered troops with the well-loved St. Crispin's Day speech.

unpopular with the English, who had been expecting to reap large amounts of ransom money for the captives.

The final French attack was no more successful than the first two, and the two French commanders were killed, effectively putting an end to the battle. Henry's weakened army of six thousand men had routed a force that was five times larger.

she said, ordered her to relieve Orléans and to have Charles VII crowned king of France in Rheims.

Firmly convinced that she was carrying out God's will, Joan won her family's compliance and made contact with a nearby military authority. She was sent to the duke of Lorraine, who recommended her to the French king. With an escort of six men-at-arms, Joan, wearing men's clothing, traveled to Chinon, where Charles VII was staying. He had already received a letter explaining the purpose of her coming, and he agreed to see her.

An ecclesiastical commission was appointed to investigate and interrogate Joan, but she passed the ordeal, and the commission made a favorable report. The king raised an army with the last of his funds, and Joan rode at its head, inspiring the soldiers with her religious fervor. They breached the blockade of Orléans in early May of 1429, and ten days later the English ended the siege.

Joan's job was still not done. Charles still needed to be crowned in Rheims, a city that was at the time held by the Burgundians. Led by the duke of Alençon, Marshal de la Hire, and Joan, the French army pushed on, encountering the English at Patay on June 19; they destroyed the enemy force entirely. Still, Joan would not let the French forces rest, and on July 17, 1429, Charles was indeed crowned in Rheims cathedral, and Joan announced that her task was ended.

At the insistence of her comrades in arms, however, Joan agreed to remain in the king's service until Paris was liberated. The attack on Paris failed, and Joan suffered a thigh wound. She continued campaigning with the French army until she was taken prisoner by the Burgundians near Compiègne in May of the following year.

Joan was handed over to the English and then transferred to Rouen, where she was tried for heresy in an ecclesiastical court presided over by Pierre Cauchon, bishop of Beauvais. The heresy charges against her were based on her claims to have had divine revelations, her refusal to obey the commands of the church, her dressing in men's clothing, and her immodesty in wearing armor and leading an army. After a long preliminary interrogation, the trial took place and Joan was forced to sign a full confession. She was handed over to the secular authorities and burned at the stake in 1431.

## The End of Hostilities

Following the loss of Orléans, Philip the Good, duke of Burgundy, realized that the English would never conquer the whole of France, and he switched sides. Under the Treaty of Arras (1435), Philip reconciled with Charles VII and agreed to withdraw from the war in exchange for Auxerre, Boulogne, and the fortresses along the Somme River. Charles agreed to condemn the murder of Philip's father, John the Fearless, and to dismiss Philip from his obligations as a vassal for life.

The English regent, the duke of Bedford, died six days before the signing of the treaty, and his two successors were unable to agree on anything. In addition, the young king, Henry VI, proved to be mentally deficient. The French army began increasingly deep incursions into English territory.

In 1436, the city of Dieppe defected to the French, and the Parisians expelled the English garrison from the French capital. Persistent guerrilla warfare gradually sapped the morale of the English occupying forces.

Weariness with the war eventually led to the Truce of Tours, which, however, did not result in a lasting peace. War broke out again when the English attacked the Francophile duke of Brittany in the 1440s.

The immediate goal of the new campaign was for the French to reconquer Normandy. In October of 1449, Rouen finally capitulated, followed by Cherbourg in August of 1450. In Aquitaine, Bayonne surrendered in 1451, and Bordeaux finally fell to the French two years later. England had lost all its possessions in France apart from Calais, and civil war at home made any attempt to recapture them impossible.

This illuminated image from Recueil des Croniques de'Engleterre, or Account of the Chronicles of England, shows a battle from the War of the Roses.

## CHAPTER NINE

# Lancaster and York: The Wars of the Roses

In the fifteenth century, rivalry between the royal houses of Lancaster and York—the two main branches of the descendants of Edward III—created civil strife that divided and weakened England for more than thirty years.

In France, Charles VII died in 1461 and was succeeded by his son, Louis XI, who ruled until 1483. King Louis concentrated on strengthening the power of the crown and extending its authority over the greater part of France. Central government gradually replaced the earlier feudal system, and French citizens began to feel loyalty to the monarch rather than to a local lord.

Meanwhile, in England, the two mighty houses of York and Lancaster were engaged in a bitter struggle for the crown. Their confrontations, which lasted from 1455 to 1485, were later dubbed the **Wars of the Roses**, after the badges associated with the two rival houses—the red rose of Lancaster and the white rose of York.

## The Sons of Edward III

The seeds of the Wars of the Roses had been sown almost a century earlier, when Edward III died in 1377. The king had several sons, including Edward (the Black Prince), Lionel (Duke of Clarence), John of Gaunt (Duke of Lancaster), and Edmund Langley (Duke of York). The Black Prince had died in battle in 1376, and it was his young son who inherited the crown as Richard II.

Richard was only ten years old when he became king. His oldest uncle, the Duke of Clarence, had died in 1368, so the power behind the throne fell to the oldest surviving uncle, John of Gaunt. On coming of age, Richard antagonized a number of his lords and ministers, including Henry Bolingbroke, John of Gaunt's son. When Gaunt died in 1399, Richard confiscated his extensive Lancastrian estates. In retaliation, Bolingbroke assembled an army, invaded England, and forced Richard to abdicate. Bolingbroke took the throne as the first Lancastrian king, Henry IV.

Henry was succeeded by his charismatic son, Henry V, who won a great victory against the French in 1415 at Agincourt and was actually designated heir to the French throne as a result. However, Henry V's success in France was cut short by his death in 1422. His infant son, not yet one year old, inherited England's throne as Henry VI.

It was at this point that the troubles really began. As Henry VI grew up, it became apparent that he was unable to provide strong leadership. In 1445, he married Margaret of Anjou, a niece of the French king, and power in the English court became polarized between two opposing factions. One faction was headed by the politically aggressive queen, who, with the dukes of Suffolk and Somerset, controlled the weak king. The other faction was headed by the powerful Richard, duke of York, who was descended from two sons of Edward III (Edmund Langley, Duke of York, and Lionel, Duke of Clarence) and thus was regarded as having a strong claim to the throne himself.

## Complaint of the Commons of Kent

Richard's supporters—known as the Yorkists—were popular with the English people, who held Margaret of Anjou responsible for the loss of territory in France. The people were upset about the mismanagement of the war in France, about ruinous taxation, and about corruption at court. In 1450, a revolt broke out in Kent. An army of twenty thousand men, with Jack Cade (a veteran soldier) at their head, marched on London to present the "Complaint of the Commons of Kent." This document demanded that several of the king's ministers should be dismissed and that reforms should be put in place to provide stable and responsible government. After the Royal Council refused to receive the document, Cade's troops defeated a royal army at Sevenoaks in Kent. However, the rebellion was short-lived, and when the government offered a pardon to those who would disperse, the insurgents melted away. Cade, however, was killed as he fled to Sussex.

Cade's Rebellion highlighted popular discontent with the royal party and strengthened the hand of the Duke of York. In 1453, Henry VI became psychologically incapable of ruling, and a council of regency was set up, with Richard, Duke of York, as lord protector. Richard took the opportunity to arrest the Duke of Somerset, his hated rival, and imprisoned him in the Tower of London. When Henry recovered early in 1455, he released Somerset, dismissed Richard, and restored the queen and her party to power.

## War Breaks Out

Richard had powerful allies in the Neville family, to whom he was related by marriage. The Earl of Salisbury and his son Richard Neville, Earl of Warwick (later to be called Warwick the Kingmaker), helped the Duke of York to raise an army, and together they confronted the king's forces at St. Albans, northwest of London, on the morning of May 22, 1455. The encounter was short and bloody. In less than an hour, Somerset was killed and the king was taken prisoner. The first battle of the Wars of the Roses had resulted in a victory for the Yorkists.

When Henry VI lost his sanity, the Duke of York took control of the government; the king retained only his title. However, the civil war had only begun. After four years of uneasy truce, hostilities resumed in 1459. At the Battle of Blore Heath in Staffordshire, a royalist army failed to stop a Yorkist force led by the earl of Salisbury on its march to join the Duke of York at Ludlow Castle. Three weeks later, however, the combined Yorkist forces were defeated by a much larger Lancastrian army at the Battle of Ludford Bridge in Ludlow. The Duke of York fled to Ireland, while his son Edward, earl of March (later to be Edward IV), together with the earls of Salisbury and Warwick, took refuge in Calais, France.

This setback for the Yorkists was only temporary. In June of 1460, the earls of Salisbury and Warwick landed with a small force in Kent

Despite being bitter enemies during the Battle of Wakefield, Warwick and Queen Margaret eventually formed an important alliance. Here, Warwick submits to helping Margaret.

and were immediately welcomed by the local population and, later, by the citizens of London. The merchants of the capital were tired of the weak government that allowed French ships to attack English ships in the English Channel, bringing trade with the Low Countries (present-day Belgium and Netherlands) to a standstill. Londoners welcomed the Yorkists and refused to contribute soldiers or money to the royalists.

From London, the Yorkists marched north, gathering new supporters as they went, and confronted the royalist army, led by Queen Margaret, on July 10, 1460. The resulting Battle of Northampton was an overwhelming victory for the Yorkists. Henry VI was captured and taken to London; the queen fled to Wales.

Emboldened by this latest military success, Richard, Duke of York, hurried back from Ireland and made a triumphal entry into

London. Richard then announced his claim to the throne and demanded that the Lancastrian king should be deposed. Although the parliament was thoroughly disillusioned with the weakness of Henry VI, it wanted strong rule, not revolution, so the parliament refused to give in to Richard's demands. In the end, a compromise was reached. Richard was made Protector of the Realm and ruled in Henry's name. In addition, Richard and his heirs were named as Henry's successors, thereby disinheriting Henry's six-year-old son.

## The Battle of Wakefield

Queen Margaret, whose main aim in the struggle between Lancaster and York had been to see her son on the throne of England, refused to give up his inheritance. She raised an army in the west and took up a position near the city of York in the north. Richard marched out of London to meet the royalist forces and established himself at Sandal Castle near Wakefield. On December 30, 1460, even though the queen's forces were reported to outnumber his own by two to one, Richard led his army out of the castle to attack. The Battle of Wakefield was a devastating defeat for the Yorkists. Richard was killed, and the Earl of Salisbury and Richard's seventeen-year-old son Edmund, Earl of Rutland, were captured and beheaded. Margaret ordered that all three heads should be displayed on pikes at the gates of York.

Margaret and her army then moved south, aiming to free Henry, who was still held captive in London. Her troops wreaked havoc as they went, looting and pillaging all before them. At St. Albans, the royalists confronted the hastily gathered forces of the earl of Warwick, and after scattering them, Margaret's army discovered King Henry sitting under a tree. Instead of continuing to London, the conquerors paused to carry out a series of bloody executions and to plunder the town of St. Albans.

It was a costly mistake. Hearing of the savagery of the queen's army, the people of London shut the city gates. Meanwhile, Edward, the new Duke of York, cut his way through a body of Lancastrians at Mortimer's Cross in Herefordshire and marched boldly on London. Joining forces with the Earl of Warwick, Edward entered London unopposed. Indeed, he was welcomed enthusiastically into the largely pro-Yorkist city.

When the bishop of London asked the citizens whom they wanted as ruler, they replied with shouts: "Long live King Edward." The handsome, vigorous nineteen-year-old was evidently a vast improvement on the decrepit, mentally unstable forty-year-old Henry.

## A New King

Edward was proclaimed king on March 4, 1461. Quickly raising an army, the new king, Edward IV, pursued the retreating Lancastrians north. The two armies, which together numbered some sixty thousand men, met on March 29 at Towton Field, near Tadcaster. At dawn, in a flurry of snow, the Yorkists attacked, and a savage battle raged for the next six hours. The Lancastrians slowly gave way, and then they were pursued, with frightful carnage, throughout the night. Thousands died on both sides, and the queen, along with her husband and son, fled to Scotland.

Edward IV

Following this devastating defeat, which saw the deaths of many of the Lancastrian leaders, some of the surviving Lancastrian nobles switched their allegiance to the new king, and those who remained loyal took refuge in the northern border areas or in Wales.

Edward was officially crowned king in London in June of 1461, and he ruled in relative peace for the next nine years. He formed a stable government, and some prosperity returned to the country as the predatory French ships in the English Channel were repulsed. The elderly King Henry was captured in 1465 and held prisoner in the Tower of London. For a time, it seemed that the dazzling "sun of York" would indeed be the savior of the country.

However, all was not well at court. The relationship between the king and Richard Neville, Earl of Warwick, deteriorated rapidly. Warwick had risen to a position of great power. He was governor of Calais, lieutenant of Ireland, and warden of the western marches. His wealth was almost immeasurable, consisting as it did of the vast estates of the earldom of Warwick, together with many Lancastrian estates awarded to him after the Battle of Towton. For a time, Neville was content to be the power behind the throne, but as the young king began to assert his independence, the relationship turned sour.

One of the main causes of the rift was the fact that, in 1464, Edward IV had contracted a secret marriage to Elizabeth Woodville. Warwick, who was keen to promote an alliance with France, had been negotiating for Edward to marry a French bride, and when the alliance with the Woodvilles became known, it caused the earl some considerable embarrassment. Edward's arranging for his sister to marry Charles the Bold of Burgundy, a sworn enemy of France, further thwarted Warwick's aim of forming a close connection with France.

Warwick became increasingly disillusioned with the young king he had put on the throne. He saw how the king's new relatives, the Woodvilles, were preferred to Warwick's own family.

## Deposing a King and Unlikely Alliances

Determined to regain his former power, Warwick formed an alliance with the king's younger brother George, Duke of Clarence, who was married to Warwick's daughter. Clarence—jealous of Edward's popularity and position as king—was happy to join forces with the Earl of Warwick. The two of them raised an army and confronted the king's forces at the Battle of Edgecote Moor on July 26, 1469. The outcome of the battle was a victory for Warwick and Clarence; Edward was captured and held as a prisoner in Middleham Castle in Yorkshire.

Warwick planned to summon a parliament at York; he hoped to get Edward deposed on the basis that he was illegitimate and to get Clarence declared king. However, Edward's loyal youngest brother Richard, Duke of Gloucester, raised an army from among royalist nobles, marched on York, and freed the king. Warwick and Clarence fled to France.

Queen Margaret was also a refugee in France, where she was trying to persuade the king, Louis XI, to help her regain the English throne for her husband, Henry VI, who was still held captive in the Tower of London. Louis proposed that Margaret should join forces with the Earl of Warwick. The suggestion was at first greeted with horror by the two old enemies, but they came to see that the idea could have benefits for both of them. Eventually, it was agreed that Warwick would attempt to free Henry and put him back on the throne of England. If Warwick succeeded, Margaret's son, the former Prince of Wales, would marry Warwick's daughter, Anne Neville.

In 1470, Warwick landed with a small force in Kent, where the local people flocked to his banner. The Lancastrians in the north rose in support of their imprisoned king, and Edward IV and the duke of Gloucester were forced to take refuge in Burgundy. Warwick entered London, released Henry VI, and restored the old king to the throne.

Edward, although exiled, was not without resources. He borrowed from the Duke of Burgundy a large sum of money that enabled him to raise a substantial army. Edward landed in Yorkshire in March of 1471. He captured York, marched unopposed to London (which he entered on April 11), and was welcomed by rejoicing citizens. Henry VI was returned to the Tower of London, and Edward IV marched northward to confront Warwick.

## Edward IV Regains the Crown

The armies of Edward and Warwick met around 10 miles (16 km) outside London on April 14, 1471. The Battle of Barnet was fought in dense fog. In the confusion, it was not always clear who was fighting whom. At one point, a Lancastrian force mistakenly attacked other Lancastrians, who then fled because they thought they had been betrayed; Warwick died in the rout.

On the same day, Queen Margaret and her son, Prince Edward, landed in the West Country. Learning of Warwick's defeat and death at Barnet, she quickly raised another army and, marching eastward, met King Edward's forces on May 4 at the Battle of Tewksbury. The encounter ended in another victory for the Yorkists. Prince Edward, the Lancastrian heir, was killed, and several Lancastrian lords were

Richard III

captured and executed. Margaret was taken prisoner.

When he returned to London on May 21, 1471, Edward ordered the death of Henry VI. The French king, Louis XI, paid a ransom for Queen Margaret, who died eleven years later in her native Anjou. Edward was restored to the throne and reigned securely until his death in 1483.

During the final years of Edward IV's reign, England enjoyed a welcome period of peace and prosperity. At court, however, tensions were mounting. The king's preferment of the Woodville family inspired jealousy in those who witnessed the queen's relatives amassing government offices, lands, and wealth. The other source of dissension emanated from George, Duke of Clarence (the king's brother), who had fought against the king at Edgecote Moor and had subsequently been forgiven. Clarence felt slighted when he saw honors heaped on his younger brother, Richard, Duke of Gloucester.

## Richard, Duke of Gloucester

Richard, Duke of Gloucester, had been loyal to Edward IV and provided valuable support when it was most needed. Now that his throne finally seemed secure, Edward awarded his brother the estates of many dead Lancastrians and made him chamberlain of England and warden of the west marches, the middle marches, and the north marches. This all made Richard the most powerful man in the kingdom after the king himself.

## The Mystery of the Two Princes

After Edward IV died in April of 1483, his twelve-year-old son became the new king, Edward V. The boy's uncle, Richard, Duke of Gloucester, who had been appointed his guardian, lodged him in the Tower of London. Edward was soon joined there by his nine-year-old brother, Richard, Duke of York. After July of that year, the two princes were never seen or heard of again.

When the Duke of Buckingham led a revolt against Richard III in September of 1483, the rebels at first demanded that Edward V should be reinstated and recognized as the rightful king. Later, however, they claimed that the two princes had been murdered by Richard III. This version of events was accepted for centuries.

Certainly, the sixteenth-century historian Thomas More believed this story. In his *History of King Richard III*, written around 1513, he describes how Richard first demanded that Robert Brackenbury, the keeper of the Tower, should kill the princes. When Brackenbury refused to do so, Richard sent James Tyrrell to do the deed. Tyrrell employed two henchmen to murder the princes in their beds. More described how the two boys were smothered with their pillows, and then their bodies were buried "at the foot of the stair, under a great heap of stones."

More claimed that Tyrrell confessed to this deed before he was executed for treason in 1502. However, More had a strong incentive to blacken Richard's reputation: he wrote the work during the reign of Henry VIII, whose father, Henry Tudor, had seized the crown from Richard.

Henry Tudor also had a motive for killing the princes. If Edward V was legitimate, then Henry had no right to the throne. It is therefore possible that the princes were killed on Henry's orders, rather than on Richard's.

*The Two Princes and Richard in the Tower*, by Sir John Everett Millais

Another theory suggests that the princes were not murdered but left the Tower in the care of their mother and grew up under false names. In support of this theory is the fact that in March of 1484, Elizabeth Woodville's daughters left sanctuary and took up residence at Richard III's court. Elizabeth would hardly have allowed her daughters to do this if she thought that Richard had murdered her sons.

In the seventeenth century, workmen discovered the skeletons of two young children in the Tower of London. It was assumed that these were the remains of the two princes, and they were reburied in Westminster Abbey. However, in 1933, the bones were exhumed and examined by a pathologist, who concluded that although they were the remains of two young children in approximately the right age ranges, it was impossible to determine the sexes.

Not surprisingly, Clarence did not receive any honors, but he nevertheless felt entitled to interfere in affairs of state. Edward became increasingly irritated by his behavior, and when, in 1477, Clarence accused the queen, Elizabeth Woodville, of witchcraft, the king had him arrested and tried for treason. He was executed in February of 1478.

The queen's family, the Woodvilles, had also risen to positions of power. The Woodville family was headed by Anthony Woodville (Earl Rivers) and Thomas Grey (Marquess of Dorset). The family had considerable influence over the young Edward, Prince of Wales; he had his own court at Ludlow, which was presided over by Rivers. When the king died suddenly in 1483, the Prince of Wales was only twelve years old. Richard, Duke of Gloucester, who had been named the protector of England by the dying king, now led the opposition to the Woodville faction.

As the new young king rode toward London with Rivers and an armed troop of men, he was kidnapped by Richard, Duke of Gloucester, at Stony Stratford in Buckinghamshire. After arresting Rivers, Richard took the king to London and locked him in the Tower. When the queen, Elizabeth Woodville, heard news of the coup, she sought sanctuary in the Palace of Westminster, together with her younger son, Richard, Duke of York. She was later persuaded to allow the nine-year-old Richard to join his brother in the Tower, and the fate of the two boys remains unknown to this day (see box, page 130).

## Richard III Becomes King

Richard, Duke of Gloucester, and his supporters dreaded the idea of another young king, with a prolonged regency and a possible return to civil war. Richard was determined to prevent such an outcome and took steps to secure the crown for himself. Rivers and other leading members of the Woodville family were executed, and William Hastings, who had been chief advisor to Edward IV, was convicted of treason and sent to the block. The two young princes were proclaimed to be illegitimate on the grounds that Edward IV's marriage to Elizabeth Woodville had been invalid.

On July 6, 1483, Richard, Duke of Gloucester, was crowned king as Richard III. The speed with which he had achieved his objective worried many observers, who remained unconvinced that the princes were illegitimate. There was also a Lancastrian claimant to the throne—Henry Tudor, Earl of Richmond. His claim was tenuous; his father had been a half brother of Henry VI, and he himself was a descendant of Edward III through his mother, Margaret Beaufort. Nevertheless, to many people he seemed preferable to someone who was patently a usurper.

In September of 1483, the Duke of Buckingham led an uprising that aimed to put Henry Tudor on the throne. The rebellion was quickly quashed, and Buckingham was executed. For the next two years, Richard III's position seemed secure, as he continued to rule a stable kingdom. However, on the continent, Henry Tudor was winning support from the French king to mount a bid for the throne of England. In August of 1485, Henry landed on the coast of Pembrokeshire with a small force and, gathering an army of supporters on his march through Wales, confronted Richard's forces at Bosworth Field in Leicestershire on August 22. Some of Richard's army defected, and Richard was killed on the field. According to legend, Henry Tudor then picked up the crown of England from a hawthorn bush, where it had fallen, and placed it on his head.

## Henry VII

Henry returned to London, where he was crowned King Henry VII. He was twenty-eight years old. The following year, to put an end to the rivalry between York and Lancaster once and for all, Henry married Elizabeth of York, the daughter of Edward IV, thereby uniting the two houses. Henry reigned until his death in 1509, bringing stability and security to his realm and establishing the great dynasty of Tudor monarchs that was to preside over England for the next one hundred years.

Philip the Bold greatly increased the power and influence of Burgundy.

CHAPTER TEN

# Burgundy Becomes Independent

The duchy of Burgundy had traditionally been one of the territories given by the king of France to his second and subsequent sons. In the fifteenth century, however, it shook off French rule and became a powerful independent state.

In the fifteenth century, a new power emerged in the area between northeastern France and northwestern Germany, on lands that had been at the center of Charlemagne's former empire. This new power was the house of Burgundy, a dynasty that had a brief but important effect on European politics.

As early as the thirteenth century, the French monarchs had arranged for each of their younger brothers to govern a large area, termed an ***apanage***. One such brother in the second half of the fourteenth century was Duke Philip the Bold, brother of King Charles V of France. His apanage included Burgundy.

Living at the time of the Hundred Years' War, Philip tried to build as strong a position as possible at the French court and at home. Although Philip was a member of the Valois family, the ruling dynasty of France, he was by no means loyal to it. Behind the scenes, he plotted actively with and against other members of the royal family, and although he always considered himself a French prince, he did not hesitate to work with the English if it suited him to do so. Philip the Bold was essentially a politician, and his successful machinations made Burgundy so powerful that it became virtually an independent state.

By marrying Margaret of Flanders, the heiress to the count of Flanders, in 1369, Philip added that county to his possessions. By virtue of the fact that he was brother to the king of France, he also obtained possession of Nevers and Franche-Comte.

Philip's son, John the Fearless (ruled 1404–1419), continued the expansion of the state. He fought with his cousin Louis, duke of Orléans, who became the regent of France when Charles VI, the brother of Louis, became unfit to rule. John plotted against both Charles and Louis, and he is thought to have been responsible for the murder of Louis in 1407.

In 1419, John the Fearless was stabbed to death on the bridge at Montereau, where he had gone to meet with the dauphin (the son of Charles VI). John's son, Philip the Good, succeeded him and continued his father's policies, supporting the claim of Henry V of England to the French throne. However, Charles VII of France and his Armagnac allies were prospering, and the English and Burgundians were put on the defensive. Philip decided to abandon the English and seek peace with France. By the Treaty of Arras (1435), peace was established between them, and in return, Charles gave up his rights as lord of Flanders and Burgundy, thereby adding greatly to Philip's domain.

## The Dream of Philip the Good

Philip the Good, whose ambitions were even greater than those of John the Fearless and Philip the Bold, dreamed of presiding over an empire between France and Germany in an area roughly equivalent to the lands granted to Lothair on the dissolution of the Carolingian Empire some six hundred years earlier.

Philip was a capable ruler and administrator. He imposed order on Flanders and Burgundy, so the aristocracy in the countryside and the merchants in the cities had a stable environment in which to conduct their affairs.

Philip's expansionist policy was most successful in the Low Countries (modern Belgium and the Netherlands), which were divided into a series of feudal kingdoms, torn by civil conflict within the aristocracy. Philip first focused his attention on Holland, Zeeland, and Hainault, where he faced minimal opposition from the indigenous population.

Philip the Good

Philip's uncle, William of Bavaria, was count of Zeeland, Holland, and Hainault. When he died, the three counties were inherited by his daughter, Jacoba of Bavaria, but her claim was not recognized by the German king, and she had to fight for her inheritance. Eventually, in 1428, she reached a settlement with Philip, under which she retained her title, but Philip became the effective ruler.

During the next twenty years, Philip added Brabant, Limburg, Namur, and Luxembourg to his realm. He also influenced the appointments of bishops in Utrecht and Liège in 1456, so that both of those church-states were governed by bishops who favored Burgundy. By the end of Philip the Good's reign, the Burgundians ruled over all of what is present-day Belgium and much of what is now the Netherlands.

## Quest for a Crown

The affluence of the Burgundians had increased in proportion to their territorial acquisitions. Philip the Good kept a magnificent court in his capital at Dijon, rivaling the flamboyance of the court of Philip the Bold, who had once served up a pie containing a complete orchestra. On feast days, fountains spouted wine for the public gathered at the palace gates. Burgundy was recognized as a cultural center, where the Burgundian women set the style for the whole of Europe in fashion and good manners.

The duke's most fervent wish, however, was for a royal crown. He longed to be on an equal footing with the kings of France and England, but he never succeeded. There were only two people who could grant Philip the Good a crown—the pope in Rome and the emperor of Germany. Neither of them encouraged Philip's coronation.

The pope could not afford to alienate the French king, who viewed the rising Burgundian power as a menace. Despite his financial problems, the French king was a more powerful friend of the church than Philip. Withholding the crown from Philip would not bring the papacy into actual conflict with Dijon, but granting it ran the risk of offending the French king.

It was not in the emperor's interest, either, to increase the power of his vassal. The German emperor was Philip's liege lord in the Netherlands, and Franche-Comte in eastern Burgundy was a fiefdom of the German Empire.

Philip had created a medium-sized state that was strategically well placed to be either a powerful ally or a powerful enemy. That state covered a little less than half the territory of the earlier empire of the Carolingian Lothair.

## Charles the Bold

Philip's heir, Charles the Bold, inherited a well-run state, consisting of Burgundy and most of the Low Countries. The treasury was full, his subjects were on the whole contented, and his authority was generally recognized. However, the realm was not unified, either politically or legally. The prudent Philip had never tried to unify his various duchies, for fear that any attempt to do so might cause a rebellion. He was careful to leave their borders alone and preserve their historic rights and privileges. However, he ensured that he and his servants all held key positions.

Charles, who reigned from 1467 to 1477, was impulsive and prepared to take greater risks than his father. The decade of his rule was a mixture of great triumphs and terrible disasters.

## Charles Takes on the Spider

Between 1461 and 1483, France was ruled by the inscrutable Louis XI, who had much in common with his great predecessor, Philip Augustus. Louis, like Philip, was not a fighter, but he was shrewd, miserly, and ruthless. In Louis, though, these characteristics were more pronounced. His contemporaries referred to the brooding, dark-clad king as the Spider.

Louis XI

The Spider rarely used direct violence, preferring to achieve his goals by means of bribery and intrigue, and he always consulted astrologers before making any major decision. Whereas Philip the Good had been able to withstand his scheming opponent, Charles the Bold could not.

At the beginning of his reign, Charles the Bold was in a strong position. Louis XI had generated considerable resentment among his people, and Philip the Good had craftily fanned the flames of insurrection. To assist the insurgents, Charles the Bold now crossed the border with his troops, and a League of General Welfare was formed to fight the French king. However, Louis was not hated quite as much as the people in Dijon wanted to believe. Although Charles managed to take Louis prisoner, the invasion soon ground to a halt. To secure his release, Louis made some important concessions, including handing over his feudal rights to Flanders.

After Charles withdrew, Louis continued to conspire against him. He incited neighboring states to take up arms against the Burgundians and encouraged resentment among Charles's subjects over the question of their taxes, which were far more onerous than they had been under Philip the Good.

Charles's foreign policy was more aggressive than his father's. He waged more wars, and at first, he prospered. He subjugated the province of Gelderland and conquered the region between his possessions in the Netherlands and Burgundy. Finally, he even persuaded the emperor, Frederick III, to offer him a royal crown.

Frederick's agreement to that proposal was conditional on the marriage of his son, Maximilian, to Charles's only child, Mary. The emperor anticipated that the union would eventually bring Burgundian territory into the German Empire.

## The Three Orders

Under the feudal system, important political and judicial matters were discussed at meetings of feudal courts. Vassals were obliged to attend these gatherings to advise their feudal lord. However, the rise of cities complicated this practice. When a ruler granted independence to a city, citizens were automatically exempted from feudal obligations. As the cities grew more powerful, they acquired money, which was something that most medieval rulers lacked.

Rulers soon saw the value of involving cities in government and began to ask citizens to help pay the cost of administration. In return, the rulers allowed citizens to participate in the political process, but because it was impossible to canvass every individual, a system of representation was developed.

The representatives at these assemblies were chosen from three groups (or orders) of the population: the nobility, the church, and the urban citizens. Peasants were excluded. By the thirteenth century, England had established an assembly known as Parliament. The most important members of Parliament were the barons, who sometimes tried to overrule the king. The king, for his part, tried to limit the assembly's power, but its importance steadily increased during the Hundred Years' War.

In France, the assembly was called the Estates General, but it never had much power. It was first summoned around 1300 by Philip the Fair, who needed the people to vote to give him money. Later monarchs tried to avoid these assemblies so that they could do as they pleased without reference to their citizens.

In the German Empire, it proved extremely difficult to establish a central assembly of the three orders. The dukes and counts had grown used to power and had no wish to share it with an urban elite. By the fourteenth century, however, some assemblies had been created that laid down rules for royalty.

It was planned to hold the coronation ceremony in Trier, a Roman city in the Rhineland. At the appointed time, the emperor and the duke entered the town with all pomp and ceremony. However, messengers sent by Louis XI of France entered the city more circumspectly, and gaining access to the emperor, they managed to convince him that Charles was unreliable. The night before the ceremony, Frederick left Trier in secret. The coronation was canceled. Charles was furious, but Maximilian and Mary had met in Trier, and they would not forget each other.

This setback did not affect Charles's expansionist policies. Burgundy had long wanted to extend its influence into Switzerland, and when various Swiss cities formed an alliance, Charles took the opportunity to lead an army into the Jura Mountains in 1476 with the intention of crushing any independence movement. The expedition soon turned into a catastrophe. Charles's knights suffered humiliating defeats at the hands of Swiss peasants armed with pikes at the battles of Grandson and Morat. The Swiss crowned their victories by seizing the Burgundian baggage train—which was a very rich haul because Charles always traveled with much of his treasure, including jewels, tapestries, and expensive works of art.

Mary of Burgundy

More troubles lay ahead in 1477. There was a rebellion in Nancy, and Charles laid siege to the city at the beginning of January in bitter weather. The Duke of Lorraine called on the French and the Swiss to assist him. When their troops arrived, the Burgundians were again defeated, and Charles himself was killed. His naked body was found two days later, frozen in the mud and half-eaten by wolves.

Charles's daughter, Mary, inherited a divided empire. The Estates General agreed to recognize her only on certain conditions, to which Mary submitted. She also confirmed all the rights and privileges of her subjects and agreed that they should never be taxed without the consent of the Estates General or other proper authorities.

In August of 1477, Mary married Maximilian, the son of the emperor Frederick III, and as a result, her possessions all became part of the Hapsburg patrimony. The marriage was a great success, both personally and politically, and they enjoyed a few happy years together. However, in 1482, Mary was killed in a riding accident, leaving Maximilian as regent for their young son, Philip the Fair.

Charles V

Philip the Fair married advantageously in 1496, pairing himself with Joanna (Juana), the daughter of the Spanish monarchs Ferdinand and Isabella. When Ferdinand died in 1516, Joanna inherited her parents' joint kingdoms of Aragon and Castile. In 1530, Philip and Joanna's son, Charles V, became the ruler of Spain as well as of Burgundy, Italy, and the German Empire.

## CHRONOLOGY

**ca. 800 CE** Population of Europe around thirty million.

**924 CE** Aethelstan becomes the first king of united England.

**1016 CE** England united with Denmark and Norway under Cnut the Great.

**1039 CE** Ferdinand I of Castile and León begins Reconquista of Iberian Peninsula.

**1060 CE** Robert Guiscard begins Norman conquest of Sicily.

**1066 CE** Norman conquest of England.

**1086 CE** Domesday survey conducted by William I in England; shows population of around one million.

**1095 CE** Pope Urban II launches First Crusade.

**1098 CE** Foundation of Cistercian monastic order.

**1100 CE** Three largest cities in Western Europe are Venice, Rome, and Pisa.

**1135 CE** Henry I dies; England split by civil war between rival claimants to throne.

**1143 CE** Alfonso I becomes first king of Portugal. Commune of Rome established.

**1154 CE** Order in England restored on accession of Henry II. Holy Roman emperor Frederick I invades Italy.

**1157 CE** Diet of Besançon increases tension between Holy Roman emperor and pope.

**1162 CE** Frederick I razes Milan.

**1167 CE** Lombard League formed in northern Italian Peninsula.

**1174 CE** Frederick I defeated by army of Lombard League at Battle of Legnano.

**1180 CE** Philip II Augustus becomes king of France.

**1198 CE** Innocent III becomes pope. Order of Teutonic Knights founded.

**1204 CE** Constantinople falls to Fourth Crusade; Latin Empire of Constantinople established.

**1208 CE** Start of crusade against Cathar heresy.

**1212 CE** Iberian forces defeat Arabs at Battle of Las Navas de Tolosa.

**1215 CE** English barons force King John to allow Magna Carta. Frederick II becomes Holy Roman emperor. Fourth Lateran Council outlaws trial by ordeal.

**1229 CE** Frederick II crowned king of Jerusalem.

**1241 CE** Mongols defeat Poles and Teutonic Knights at Battle of Liegnitz.

**1250 CE** Population of Europe reaches between seventy million and one hundred million.

**1260 CE** Iceland becomes part of Norwegian Empire.

**1261 CE** Fall of Latin Empire of Constantinople.

**1265 CE** Rebel baron Simon de Montfort defeated by Prince Edward at Battle of Evesham in England.

**1282 CE** Thousands of French people murdered in Palermo in massacre known as the Sicilian Vespers.

**1283 CE** Edward I of England completes conquest of Wales; builds castles to solidify position.

**ca.1300 CE** Population of England around six million.

**1302 CE** Christian armies lose last stronghold in Holy Land.

**1309 CE** Papacy moves from Rome to Avignon.

**1314 CE** Poor harvests and famines begin reducing European population.

**1331 CE** Swabian League of Cities formed.

**1337 CE** Start of Hundred Years' War between England and France.

**1346 CE** English forces defeat French at Battle of Crécy.

**1347 CE** Black Death reaches Europe; around one-third of population dies over next five years.

**1356 CE** Major English victory over France at Battle of Poitiers.

**1360 CE** Treaty of Bretigny on terms favorable to English.

**1367 CE** Edward III invades France again.

**1369 CE** Burgundy and Flanders join forces through marriage of respective rulers.

**1377 CE** Edward III dies; succeeded by grandson, Richard II, as king of England.

**1378 CE** Ciompi workers rebel in Florence.

**1380 CE** Growing civil unrest in England and France leads to suspension of hostilities in Hundred Years' War.

**1381 CE** Peasants' Revolt in England.

**1382 CE** Moscow captured by Mongols of the Golden Horde.

**1399 CE** English king Richard II deposed by Henry IV.

**1410 CE** Combined forces of Poland and Lithuania defeat Teutonic Knights at Battle of Tannenberg.

**1415 CE** Council of Constance reunites western church. English triumph over French at Battle of Agincourt.

**1429 CE** English siege of Orléans lifted by Joan of Arc.

**1435 CE** Burgundy and France make peace with Treaty of Arras.

**1453 CE** English forced back to Calais; end of Hundred Years' War.

**1455 CE** Yorkists win Battle of St. Albans at start of Wars of the Roses.

**1461 CE** English king Henry VI deposed; succeeded by cousin, Edward IV.

**1470 CE** Henry VI restored to English throne.

**1471 CE** Earl of Warwick killed at Battle of Barnet; Henry VI dies; Edward IV returns to throne.

**1477 CE** Burgundians defeated by French and Swiss forces at siege of Nancy.

**1479 CE** Aragon and Castile united by Ferdinand and Isabella. Final phase of Reconquista of Iberia.

**1481 CE** Formalization of confederacy that forms basis of modern Switzerland.

**1485 CE** English king Richard III dies at Bosworth Field.

**1488 CE** Great Swabian League formed.

**1496 CE** Philip the Fair of Burgundy marries daughter of Spanish monarchs.

**1530 CE** Coronation of Holy Roman emperor Charles V unites Burgundy, Spain, and German Empire under single ruler.

# GLOSSARY

**Almohads** Islamic reformers from northern Africa who drove the Almoravids out of southern Spain in 1146 CE, establishing a strong caliphate.

**Almoravids** Muslim tribe from the southern Sahara who conquered northern Africa and aided the Muslims in Córdoba against the Christians between 1086 and 1146 CE.

***apanage*** Region in the French Empire controlled by the younger brothers of the French king. Burgundy was an apanage until the Hundred Years' War.

**Aragon** Christian kingdom in northeastern Spain, south of the Pyrenees.

**Babylonian Captivity** Fourteenth-century period when the popes resided in Avignon because Italy was divided by feuds among noblemen.

**Berbers** Descendants of the pre-Arab inhabitants of northern Africa.

**Black Death** Plague that originated in Asia and ravaged Europe between 1347 and 1351, killing around one-third of the population.

**Burgundy** Region of eastern France that became a powerful independent state in the fifteenth century.

**Byzantium** Ancient Greek city on the shore of the Bosporus; later known as Constantinople; modern Istanbul.

**Calais** Port on the north coast of France; conquered by the English king Edward III after the Battle of Crécy in 1346; remained an English bridgehead on the mainland of Europe until the sixteenth century.

**caliphate** Office and realm held by a caliph.

**Carthusians** Monastic order that stressed penance, solitude, and asceticism; founded at the end of the eleventh century CE.

**Castile** Originally a Christian kingdom in northern Spain; in the eleventh century CE, annexed León and spread Castilian culture throughout the Iberian Peninsula.

**Cathars** Heretical Christian sect that flourished in Western Europe in the twelfth and thirteenth centuries, believed that there are two principles, one good and one evil, and that the material world is evil.

**Ciompi Rebellion** Uprising of Florentine workers in the woolen industry in 1378.

**Cistercians** Monastic order founded in 1098 CE in France; concentrated on manual labor.

**Concordat of Worms** Compromise in 1122 CE between Pope Calixtus II and Holy Roman Emperor Henry V on investiture.

**Constance, Council of** Council (1414–1418) that ended the schism and forced a number of popes to abdicate.

**Constantinople** Name for Byzantium (present-day Istanbul), which became the (Christian) residence of the emperor Constantine in 330 CE. In 395 CE, it became the capital of the eastern Roman Empire.

**Crécy** Town near the northern coast of France; site where the French army, consisting of knights, was destroyed in 1346 by the English infantry, opening the way for Edward III to conquer Calais.

**crusades** Christian military expeditions from the end of the eleventh century to the end of the thirteenth century CE, primarily to wrest the Holy Land from Muslim control.

**Danegeld** Direct tax introduced by Aethelred the Unready, an Anglo-Saxon king; paid as annual tribute to the Vikings (Danes).

**Domesday Book** Land registry in which all property of the inhabitants of England was registered for tax purposes; introduced during the reign of William I.

**First Crusade (1095–1099 CE)** Led by Godfrey of Bouillon and Raymond of Toulouse; conquered Edessa, Tripoli, Antioch, and Jerusalem, making them Christian kingdoms.

**Flanders** Region on the North Sea coast; made part of Charlemagne's empire in the ninth century CE. In the eleventh century CE, the counts of Flanders were vassals for both the French crown and the Holy Roman Empire.

**Fourth Crusade (1202–1204)** Expedition by French knights; captured Byzantium with the aid of Venice and founded a western-style empire.

**Ghibellines (Waiblingen)** Supporters of the House of Hohenstaufen and proponents of the rule of a strong Holy Roman emperor over the church; ultimately defeated by the Guelphs.

**Great Swabian League** Alliance between the cities of Swabia, the Rhineland, Bavaria, and Franconia; formed under the protection of the emperor Frederick III in 1488.

**Guelphs (Welfs)** Proponents of a monarchy with little influence, powerful vassals, and an autonomous church. From 1125 CE, they fought the Ghibellines and eventually defeated the last scion of the Hohenstaufen family.

**guilds** Organizations of merchants and artisans; supervised working conditions and the quality and price of manufacture. Only guild members were allowed to practice in the cities.

**Hanseatic League** Union of free cities in northern Germany that promoted their own interests in trade; formed in the twelfth century.

**Hohenstaufens** German dynasty that ruled the Holy Roman Empire for much of the twelfth and thirteenth centuries.

**Holy Roman Empire** Mainly comprised of German states, by 1100 CE, the empire included the kingdoms of Italy, Bohemia, Burgundy, and Germany. It lasted until 1806.

**Hundred Years' War (1337–1453)** War between France and England, which still possessed areas in France about the succession to the French throne. By 1453, England had lost all territory in France except for Calais.

**interdict** Papal sanction whereby citizens of the territory of a sinner are excluded from all religious ceremonies.

**investiture** Dispute over the appointment of clergy by lay people. It was resolved in favor of the church at the Concordat of Worms in 1122 CE.

**Jacquerie** Farmers' rebellion in 1358 led by "Les Jacques," peasants in the region surrounding Paris, against their lords after years of oppression and their defeat by the English at Poitiers; finally crushed by Charles II.

**Knights Hospitallers** Society of Christian knights who fought Muslims. The order grew out of the eleventh-century-CE pilgrims' hospital in the Holy Land. When noblemen of the brotherhood became the leaders, the order took on a military character.

**Knights Templar** Religious military order established at the time of the crusades to protect Christian pilgrims to the Holy Land. The order was destroyed by King Philip IV of France in 1307.

**León** Tenth-century CE Christian kingdom in northwestern Spain; absorbed by Castile in the eleventh century CE.

**Lombard League** Alliance of Italian cities that rebelled against Frederick I Barbarossa in 1167 CE after he revoked their royal privileges. Defeated Frederick in 1176 CE.

**Lombards** Central European Germanic people; conquered most of Italy in 568 CE, leaving Byzantine rule only on the coast and in the south. The Lombard Empire was subjected by Charlemagne in the eighth century CE.

**Magna Carta** Document—issued by King John under pressure from his barons in 1215—that set down the rights and obligations of king and barons and formed the basis of political evolution in England.

**monastery** Ascetic community of monks led by an abbot under strict regulations.

**Mongols** Asian tribes of horsemen who originally came from lands to the north of China; united by Genghis Khan in 1190 CE.

**Navarre** Christian kingdom in northern Spain.

**Normandy** Area in western Gaul given in fief to the Normans in 911 CE. Norman nobles established a kingdom in southern Italy and Sicily in the early eleventh century CE. In 1204, Normandy was incorporated into the French Empire.

**Normans** Nordic people (Danes, Norwegians, and Swedes) who variously raided, traded, and settled on the coasts of Europe, Greenland, and North America in the eighth and ninth centuries CE.

**Orléans** City in the French duchy of Berry on the side of Charles VII and beleaguered by the English in 1428 and 1429. In 1429, the city was freed by a French army led by Joan of Arc.

**Peasants' Revolt** Uprising of English laborers in 1381 against taxation and the maximum wage.

**podesta** A hired strongman used by Frederick I Barbarossa against Lombard cities.

**Poitiers** City in central France; site where Edward the Black Prince of England destroyed the French army in 1356 and John the Good, the French king, was taken prisoner.

**Portugal** Western region of the Iberian Peninsula given to Henry of Burgundy and his wife, Theresa, by Alfonso I, king of Castile, in 1093 CE. The kingdom gained papal recognition in 1179 CE.

**Reconquista** Christian reconquering of Muslim-occupied Spain (eleventh–thirteenth centuries CE).

**schism** Fourteenth-century CE division in the church that occurred when the cardinals elected Clement VII as pope because they disliked Urban VI. During this time, there were two popes, one in Avignon and one in Rome.

**Sicilian Vespers** Rebellion in 1282 CE by the Sicilians against French rule. During the uprising, all Frenchmen in Palermo were killed. Sicily offered the crown to Peter of Aragon.

**simony** Sale of church offices to the highest bidder.

**Teutonic Knights** Order of knights in northern Germany and the Baltic states. Founded in 1198 CE, they were defeated at the Battle of Tannenberg in 1410. By the end of the fifteenth century, they had lost their political influence.

**Third Crusade (1187–1192 CE)** Frederick I Barbarossa, Philip II Augustus, and Richard the Lionheart traveled to Palestine. Conquered the fortress of Acre, but Jerusalem remained in Turkish hands.

**Wars of the Roses (1455–1485)** Series of dynastic civil wars between the houses of Lancaster and York, for the English throne.

# MAJOR HISTORICAL FIGURES

**Aethelstan** First king of a united England; ruled between 924 and 939 CE.

**Alfonso I** First king of Portugal; ruled between 1139 and 1185 CE; conquered Lisbon from the Muslims (1147 CE); secured Portuguese independence from León (1139 CE).

**Alfonso III** King of Portugal from 1248 to 1279; recaptured the Algarve from the Muslims.

**Arnold of Brescia (ca. 1100–1155 CE)** Preacher who criticized the church's political power. His sermons caused a rebellion in Rome in 1146 CE, after which the senate regained its power. Pope Hadrian IV and Frederick I Barbarossa conspired to have Arnold executed.

**Becket, Thomas** Archbishop of Canterbury (1162–1170 CE); opponent of Henry II, who took away the authority of the ecclesiastical courts; murdered in 1170 CE.

**Charlemagne** Frankish king from 768 to 814 CE; founded the Holy Roman Empire, of which he was emperor from 800 CE.

**Cnut (died 1035 CE)** Danish king who united Denmark, England, and Norway into a single kingdom.

**Edward III** King of England from 1327 to 1377; proclaimed himself king of France in 1337, thus sparking the Hundred Years' War; reshaped the English army into archers and lancers instead of heavily armed horsemen.

**El Cid (ca.1043–1099 CE)** El Cid Campeador (The Lord Champion); born Rodrigo Díaz de Vivar; great Spanish warrior.

**Eleanor of Aquitaine (ca.1122–1204 CE)** Heiress to the region of Aquitaine. When Louis VII of France had their marriage annulled, Eleanor married Henry II of England, giving him the western part of the French Empire.

**Frederick I (Barbarossa)** Holy Roman emperor between 1152 and 1190 CE; as a scion of the Hohenstaufen family, made peace with the Guelph leader, Henry of Saxony; removed many privileges from the princes and dukes of his realm; fought against the Lombard League, Guelphs, and pope; died during the Third Crusade.

**Frederick II** Holy Roman emperor between 1215 and 1250;

supported by Pope Innocent III; left the German noblemen to their own devices and harshly ruled the kingdom of Sicily; became king of Jerusalem in 1229.

**Henry II** First Plantagenet king of England; ruled between 1154 and 1189 CE; acquired the western part of the French Empire through his marriage to Eleanor of Aquitaine.

**Hugh Capet** King of France between 987 and 996 CE; gradually unified the previously fragmented country. The Capetian dynasty that he founded endured until 1328.

**Hus, Jan (1372–1415)** Czech religious reformer; convicted of heresy at the Council of Constance and burned at the stake.

**Joan of Arc (1412–1431)** French peasant who broke the English siege of Orléans and had Charles VII crowned king of France; captured by the English and burned at the stake as a heretic.

**Montfort, Simon de (ca.1208–1265)** Leader of the baronial revolt against King Henry III of England.

**Philip II Augustus** Ruled France 1180 and 1223 CE; annexed French territories that had previously been apportioned to the English king; instituted a nonfeudal government; forged the French kingdom into a powerful unity.

**Richard I (the Lionheart)** King of England; ruled between 1189 and 1199 CE; took part in the Third Crusade; warred against Philip II Augustus of France.

**Robert Guiscard (ca.1015–1085 CE)** Duke of Apulia and extended Norman rule over Naples, Calabria, and Sicily; laid the foundations of the kingdom of Sicily.

**William I (the Conqueror)** Ruled between 1066 and 1087 CE; defeated King Harold at the Battle of Hastings; established a centralized monarchy, granting estates to loyal followers but retaining power; ordered the compilation of the Domesday Book.

# FOR FURTHER INFORMATION


## BOOKS

Abulafia, David (ed.). *Italy in the Central Middle Ages.* New York: Oxford University Press, 2004.

Balazs, Gyorgy, and Karoly Szelenyi (translated by Zsuza Béres). *The Magyars: The Birth of a European Nation.* Budapest, Hungary: Intl Specialized Book Service Inc, 1989.

Duby, Georges (translated by Juliet Vale). *France in the Middle Ages, 987–1460: From Hugh Capet to Joan of Arc.* Cambridge, MA: Wiley-Blackwell, 1991.

Kelly, John. *The Great Mortality: An Intimate History of the Black Death, the Most Devastating Plague of All Time.* New York: Harper Perennial, 2005.


## WEBSITES

**Avignon Papacy**
www.the-orb.net/textbooks/nelson/avignon.html

**Berbers**
i-cias.com/e.o/berbers.htm

**Cathars**
www.languedoc-france.info/12_cathars.htm

**Magna Carta**
www.bl.uk/treasures/magnacarta/index.html

**Wars of the Roses**
www.warsoftheroses.com

# INDEX

Page numbers in **boldface** are illustrations. Entries in **boldface** are glossary terms.